CIRCULAR BREATHING

Meditations From a Musical Life

Praise for Circular Breathing

"It takes more than candor to find the story amidst the miscellany of one's life and give it shape and significance. Ann McCutchan, who knows that all meaning begins in the particular, uses her rich experience as a musician to meditate on art, memory, loss and desire with wit and insight. When she writes of 'sculpting the sentences of music,' I want to turn that around to say that, in this generous and inviting collection, she 'sculpts music into sentences.'"
—Rosellen Brown, author of *Tender Mercies* and *Before and After*

"Ann McCutchan's essays show gifts rarely seen in combination. They reveal a savvy, witty, worldly feel for human motivation, a lyrical appreciation of nature, and, perhaps most notably, a profoundly informed understanding of the places where music and literature meet."
—Emily Fox Gordon, author of *Mockingbird Years: A Life In and Out of Therapy* and *Are You Happy?: A Childhood Remembered*

"McCutchan's personal essays about the role of music in her life go behind the typical 'liner note' style of music writing to something far more elemental, primitive, bodily—and, hence, spiritual. In her essay, 'Opening,' she speaks of the 'windy gush of vowels,' those sounds that pry apart that in us which would otherwise be clamped shut. As a clarinetist, McCutchan has learned how music can be a spiritual as well as artistic discipline. She celebrates the beauty of music (as well as the human mind and body), interrogates her own life to discover the path she's been walking, and bears witness to the presence of mystery. That makes her a triple threat."
—*Image*

CIRCULAR BREATHING
Meditations From a Musical Life

Ann McCutchan

SUNSTONE PRESS
SANTA FE

© 2011 by Ann McCutchan.
All Rights Reserved.

No part of this book may be reproduced in any form or by any electronic or mechanical means including information storage and retrieval systems without permission in writing from the publisher, except by a reviewer who may quote brief passages in a review.

Sunstone books may be purchased for educational, business, or sales promotional use. For information please write: Special Markets Department, Sunstone Press, P.O. Box 2321, Santa Fe, New Mexico 87504-2321.

Book and Cover design ❧ Vicki Ahl
Body typeface ❧ Bernhard Modern Std
Printed on acid free paper

Library of Congress Cataloging-in-Publication Data

McCutchan, Ann.
  Circular breathing : meditations from a musical life / by Ann McCutchan.
       p. cm.
  ISBN 978-0-86534-749-6 (softcover : alk. paper)
 1. McCutchan, Ann. 2. Lyricists--United States--Biography. 3. Musicians--United States--Biography. I. Title.
  ML423.M4323A3 2011
  780.92--dc22
  [B]
                            2011013054

WWW.SUNSTONEPRESS.COM
SUNSTONE PRESS / POST OFFICE BOX 2321 / SANTA FE, NM 87504-2321 /USA
(505) 988-4418 / ORDERS ONLY (800) 243-5644 / FAX (505) 988-1025

FOR MARY

CONTENTS

Prelude—9
Acknowledgements—11
Opening—13
Green Cove—26
How I Got My Southern Accent—36
Circular Breathing—49
Five Sketches With B—73
Three Bagatelles—96
Aftermath—107
Reaching for the End of Time—113
Love From Afar—135
Second Acts—149

❧ PRELUDE ☙

A collection of literary meditations, like a musical composition bearing the same description, is not necessarily linear, but often wanders, following the mind's movements and roaming overlapping territories. To guide the reader through the course of this book, I have supplied inclusive dates for each chapter, although each is made to stand alone.

The reader might also enjoy knowing that, because I write out of the world of music, musical gestures, forms, and other elements naturally influence the shapes and moods my pieces take. For example, Circular Breathing, a meditation in three parts, was conceived as a solo concerto, beginning, in musical terms, with an *andante* movement (walking tempo), shifting to *lacrimoso* (tearfully, sadly), and finishing with a *moderato espressivo* (moderate tempo, with expression). Five Sketches With B, written in five parts, was inspired by the clarinet and piano composition *Five Sketches for Ann*, revealed in the meditation to be a musical story in five movements. And Love From Afar is a personal riff on the comic opera, including two characters who represent aspects of myself: the Perfectly Eligible Woman Who Will Never Meet Her Match and the general manager, an update of the major-domo, or household manager, in operas by composers such as Mozart and Strauss.

Pieces in this book were published previously in *Image* (Opening, Reaching for the End of Time); the *Florida Review*

(Green Cove); *Boulevard* (How I Got My Southern Accent, Circular Breathing, Five Sketches With B); the *Rochester Democrat & Chronicle* and the *Austin American-Statesman* (Three Bagatelles); the *Cimarron Review* (Aftermath); *The Bloomsbury Review* (Second Acts). Reaching For the End of Time was included in *The Best American Spiritual Writing 2007* (Houghton Mifflin). Some pieces have been revised slightly since they first appeared, and the names of some individuals have been changed.

ACKNOWLEDGEMENTS

Warm thanks to my trusted reader and friend Pat Alexander, always, amazingly on call, as well as Emily Fox Gordon and Joyce Morgenroth, and, over the years: Joan Kalisch, Linda Huggins, Kathy Allen-Weber, Joseph Squier, Mary Gilliland, Nancy Andrew, Julene Bair, Chavawn Kelley, Maija Devine, Barbara Rodman, John Tait, Amos Magliocco, Bridget Bem, and Stephanie Hawkins—insightful readers and friends, all. Special thanks to my friend and colleague Bonnie Friedman for final, invaluable advice as the manuscript inched toward the door.

My gratitude also to the Rockefeller Foundation, the MacDowell Colony, and the Hambidge Center for Creative Arts and Sciences, for precious time and ideal conditions to write.

❦ OPENING ❦

1958–1971

Krsti Fschr. Krst Fshr? Whenever Krysti Fischer spelled out her name, she omitted most of the vowels, couldn't or didn't bother to write them. My second grade classmate's phonetic handicap revealed itself when I caught the chicken pox and missed a whole week of school. Miss Olsen assigned the class a writing exercise, a get-well letter to me. Three days into my convalescence, a thick manila envelope arrived by way of a trustworthy fourth-grader who lived one street over in Bel-Air, the south Florida housing development where my family lived. I was napping in the bedroom I shared with my younger sister, breathing from the open jalousie windows the mild sea breeze of late October when my tall mother swept in, waving a sheaf of gray paper lined wide for the nubs of fat pencils. "The whole class wrote to you!" she announced with typical good cheer. "The whole class!"

I sat up and arranged my crawling skin in the bed chair, a contraption of pink paisley canvas and aluminum tubing that dug at the base of my spine. There were seventeen letters, all beginning the same way: "We are sorry you are sick. We miss you. Please get well soon." I could see pretty Miss Olsen chalking this on the green board, my classmates dutifully copying it down.

Anything they wrote after that message was original.

dr Ann,
M srr sck. W Ms pls gt ll sn. N I mr hns 2 ws.
Krsti Fschr

  Like the first time I witnessed a child seize up with epilepsy, or a blind man strike the sidewalk with a cane, Krysti's infirmity seared the tender spot beneath my breastbone with a fresh awareness of pain, struggle, limits. When I returned to school, I thanked Krysti for the message I could not decipher and began to pay more attention to her. Krysti sat on the opposite side of the room and belonged to the slowest reading group. When Miss Olsen asked a question, she never raised her hand. One day at lunch I listened as Krysti communicated with a child from another class. It was the first time I had heard her speak a sentence, and the words lurched out of her in vowel-less knots, as if all of the physical and intellectual circuits involved in pronouncing, say, "hamburger," were jammed in her throat. Only by sheer will could she force a word past her tongue, teeth and lips: MBRGR.

  Vowels open the throat, the head, the chest, every part of the body that resonates, that creates true voice. When vocalists warm up before a concert, they sing Aaay, Eeee, Ahhh, Ohhh, Oooo. Instrumentalists think about opening their throats, forming Ahhh or Ohhh behind their mouthpieces to render tones rich with full, chiming partials. Once a player has produced an open airstream he can articulate on its flow, forming the equivalents of consonants by tonguing the reed or buzzing the mouthpiece, sculpting the sentences of music.

Without the windy gush of vowels, the instrument dies, the musician is gagged, like Papageno in *The Magic Flute*, who, when his lips are padlocked, utters only Mm. Even in popular culture, a string of consonants betokens misfortune. My second-grade comic book hero Superman was tormented by Mr. Mxyzptlk, a bald-headed leprechaun who wreaked havoc on the city of Metropolis. Physically, Mr. Mxyzptlk was far less threatening than Superman's chief nemesis Lex Luthor, but his vowel-starved name struck terror, even before you encountered his impish image. It was as if Mr. Mxyzptlk lacked an essential human feature, like saliva or fingernails or veins.

There are languages which, when written down, contain few vowels or vowel equivalents. Hebrew contains no vowels at all, and so, for example, the ancient Hebraic name of God, which was considered too sacred to speak, is spelled YHWH. It comes from the verb "to be," it means "I am." To pronounce YHWH you must connect the consonants with unnotated vowels, and because no one knows the correct pronunciation of the sacred, silent word, you must improvise the open sounds, name God for yourself.

Vowels are galleries of air shaped by the lancet arches of consonants. They are the fickle drafts against which stiff kites play, trampolines that send Fs and Js and Ts bouncing into the next A-E-I. Vowels pillow fricatives. Pliant as taffy, they are the source of all accents. Tissue, not bone; plain, not mountain. Vowels puff and sigh and howl us into what's beyond and give our throats a place to rest, as well.

Krysti Fisher had a speech defect and probably a learning

disability not easily remedied in the 1950s. Tall for her age, with a boxy frame and a Joan of Arc haircut, she moved about our classroom with exquisite care, as if fearing to knock over the chalk carton, or the guinea pig's cage, or the rolling cart of hideous clay ashtrays we formed and fired for our parents. After the second grade, I glimpsed her only from a distance because the lottery determining class membership failed to toss us into the same company of children.

In the fourth grade I encountered another child with an irregular voice. Round-headed Burney Gray, a mama's boy, was blessed with an astonishingly high soprano that soared each morning during The Star Spangled Banner, winning giggles from his fellow nine year-olds and the admiration of our teacher, Mrs. Chapman, an elderly Cracker with moist blue eyes who graded easy and read to us from Marjorie Kinnan Rawlings' *The Yearling* every day after lunch. Burney knew his voice was beautiful and hilarious, and he enjoyed the attention he won on both counts. His notoriety withered, though, when a bad boy named Greg jabbed him in the eye with the end of a broom handle. For weeks the white of Burney's right eye glared red with blood, and though Greg insisted it was an accident, most of us knew better. After school, Burney's mother confronted Greg's as Mrs. Chapman attended them, aloof and docile in her faded housedress. There were no apologies. The next morning during the national anthem, Burney's lips were sealed.

Soon afterward, my First Bra ritual took place, nearly two years before the other girls in my class. Boys like Greg made fun, and I grew shy. I stopped raising my hand. In January, Mrs. Holbrook, the music teacher who appeared weekly with boxes of song books, rhythm sticks and tambourines, invited interested fourth graders to learn a black plastic flute-like instrument called a Tonette. The Tonette cost $1.25, its music fifty cents. I cracked open my glass piggy bank to get the money, and with Burney Gray, joined the McNab Elementary School Tonette Band.

To discover an alternate voice when you've set aside your original is better than a new bike, a pony, or even a boyfriend. I latched onto the Tonette as if it were a missing part of my body, because in a way, it was. So did Burney. In Tonette class, we both grew bold again, claiming desks in front. Burney knew how to read music, but I did not, and so I acquired the new language by myself, taking pleasure in the correspondence between first line "F" and the waffling pitch I produced by covering the Tonette's lone underside tone-hole with my left thumb and blowing lightly into the thin slot of the mouthpiece. It was easy to overblow the Tonette, to send up an erratic mess of overtones that sounded the way a sheaf of paper looks when the wind scatters it. On thumb F, I began to learn the art of gentle, consistent breathing. Adding my left forefinger to the first hole on the upper side of the Tonette got me first line E. Then another finger, and another, D, C, B, A, down to the lowest note on the Tonette, another, deeper F, all fingers down, all holes covered.

On the Tonette or any other wind instrument, all notes are, in a sense, vowels, rousing a trunk full of air and the kaleidoscopic effects on the wood or metal it sets to humming. Musical sounds are abstract, open as wide as A or O to use and interpretation.

The 18th-century Christian mystic Jean-Pierre de Caussade told the Visitation nuns of Nancy, "we must have a great deal of simplicity, a gentle cheerfulness, and we must also respond at once to the breath of grace. We must let ourselves go, ready and eager to obey our impulses, for God never fails to give us guidance . . ."

When you push air from the pulsing deep bin of your body into the waiting column of a cured wood instrument, a kind of grace may sweep up along with it, tending to the letting go. It is in this moment that a child knows she must keep doing this thing, at whatever cost, that the making of music with the body is grace. It is the whoosh of life she has longed for, the open door, the wide horizon. Though she'll face it again, she believes it is possible that the choke, the pinch, will loosen.

Burney and his family moved away over the summer, leaving me alone in my growing desire to play a real instrument. For some reason, McNab Elementary offered little music to ten year-olds, and Mrs. Holbrook's weekly appearances were often preempted by visits from the school nurse, who delivered lectures on hygiene. These were not thinly disguised discussions about menstruation and wet dreams, but tiresome lectures about soap and water. I bought my first jar of Mum cream deodorant after one of those sessions. But what I recall most about hygiene class was listening to the sixth grade beginning band play in the cafeteria nearby. Such a relief it was, to let my mind wander off the subject of dress shields and dental floss and plunge it into the majestic wheeze of flutes, clarinets, saxophones, trumpets and trombones, pressing out the tones of the B-flat major scale like a room-sized accordion.

It was around this time that my mother began buying classical music records for ninety-nine cents each at the Fort Lauderdale A & P. I remember what she put in the shopping cart to earn that low, low price: Jane Parker apple pie, hard as a hubcap; Spanish Bar Cake, coated with white frosting you could peel off like a wig; Ann Page peanut butter, its label stamped with the portrait of the ideal housewife—face polished pink, hair neatly bobbed. But then came the records: Ferde Grofé's *Grand Canyon Suite*, Bedrich Smetana's *Die Moldau*, Antonin Dvorak's *New World Symphony*. I can see the albums stacked at the end of the canned meat aisle, luring beach-blind buyers of Hormel Vienna Sausages with soothing cover photographs of mountains, rivers, and forests. The albums did not fit into the brown paper grocery bags, so I was invited each week to carry the new record to the back seat of our round-rumped Hudson sedan and gaze at it on the way home. Once we had pulled into the double garage, I would jump out of the Hudson, carry my prize past the Styrofoam surfboards in the utility room, on through the turquoise kitchen and the plant-filled Florida Room to the living room where the Magnavox stereo—a hunk of mahogany battened with waffle-weave speaker cloth—stood. I would draw the new record from its cover and work it onto the greased spindle so that it dropped straight down onto the turntable with a soft plop. Then I would press the "on" button, lift the tone arm, and poise the stylus over the wide outer groove, waiting for the gleaming disk to reach maximum speed.

    Oh, and once the needle settled into the spinning rings of perfect vinyl, achieved the delicate friction required to release the necklaces of song submerged in the oily platter, I could attach my own thoughts and feelings to the violins that soared, the trumpets that flourished, the bells that pealed. This music—played, no doubt, by cash-poor orchestras grateful for the grocery chain's contract—represented everything I wished I could express. What would I have said, had Mozart and Schubert and Beethoven not spoken for me? Everything from No One is Sadder Than I Am/Will Anybody Ever Love Me/I Am The Center of The Universe—to all of the things that cannot be put into words but together mean something beyond the inadequate "God." This is the way it is for some musicians, the kind I would be someday.

Mrs. Holbrook reappeared the next year to ask who wanted to join the beginning band, and a week later several of us trundled down the sandy porticoes of McNab to the cafeteria, where a middle-aged man with a baton wiggling in his back pocket took our names and instrument preferences. At the time I was under the spell of a bossy girl named Pamela who lived in an oceanfront development with a guardhouse. Pamela chose the clarinet because her big sister Blair played one, and I chose the clarinet so I could sit next to Pamela. The clarinet was the only band instrument I had ever seen up close, because one of my babysitters, a high school girl, had shown me hers. I had been fascinated with its vertical maze of silver keys, the asymmetrical chain-link laid out like found objects on a branch of black wood.

A few days later my mother signed the rental agreement for a plastic clarinet that came with a white handkerchief swab, two Rico brand cane reeds in cardboard sleeves, a tube of gummy cork grease and a carrying case lined in red fake velvet and smelling of camphor. The band director showed us how to assemble the parts of the instrument from the bottom up: bell, lower joint, upper joint, barrel, mouthpiece. Then with one hand we neatly set a flat cane reed against the rails framing the opening of the mouthpiece, and with the other hand, brought the metal hoop of the ligature down around the reed's hips, securing it with the ligature screws. "Now, blow," said the band director, and I did, and nothing came out, nothing but Pppfffffff.

It took me days to produce anything close to a characteristic clarinet tone. When I finally barked an open G, I jumped from the impact of the sound and the physical effort it took to play that one note. But soon I learned to breathe properly for the new instrument, to pull in more than a cubic foot of air in one thrilling swoop, then release it in a consistent, malleable stream through the clarinet's mouthpiece, causing the reed to vibrate smartly like the wing of a hummingbird.

Pam and I mastered the F Major scale from thumb F down to low F, a deep, chocolaty note which required covering all six tone holes and depressing the lowest, furthest paddle key with the little finger of the right hand. It was easiest, the band director told us, to start at the head of the stairs and work down to the basement, as on the Tonette. For thumb F you fill only the topmost inches of the instrument, but for low F you imagine propelling air all the way down to the silver ring of the clarinet's bell. "Aim for the ring," he said, and we did.

What causes a clarinet to squeak, to squawk, to guffaw like a parrot? Often it's a bad seal: fingers failing to cover the tone holes completely, embouchure—the arrangement of teeth, lips, mouthpiece—lax and leaking air. Clarinetists love to blame bloopers on the reed—not *my* fault! One of the most common post-partum defenses against aborted clams is to jerk the instrument out of the mouth and frown publicly at the mouthpiece. With enough measures rest in the music, you can even afford to put one hand on your hip and sigh. Equipment does fail us, but not as often as our bodies do. Playing an instrument is a physical skill, and no matter how innately expressive we may be, disciplined form and mature eye-hand coordination are prerequisites for the dreams of Mendelssohn and Berlioz.

Many years ago I taught clarinet to a young woman who was legally blind. Her prescription eyewear resembled a pair of binoculars fastened to her ears with small handlebars, and when she played from a sheet of music, her entire body swiveled slowly left to right, following closely the trail of black specks. At the end of each line the young woman paused several seconds to swing her torso back to the left in preparation for the next staff of notes. "I want to be in an orchestra someday," she told me, and finally I broke the news: "I am sorry," I said. "Unless you are playing by yourself, the music will always run away from you."

When the handsome artist Will Ladislaw first encounters high-minded Dorothea Brooke in *Middlemarch*, he remarks to himself that Miss Brooke must be "an unpleasant girl," as she intends to marry the dry old scholar Casaubon. "But what a voice!" he exclaims inwardly, and the narrator continues, "It was like the voice of a soul that had once lived in an Aeolian harp . . ."

Dedicating yourself to music can be, for a time, like marrying Mr. Casaubon. Study and practice come before all else and erotic energy sometimes converts to prolonged yearning, feeding passionate performances and perhaps more study. I can't pretend that Miss Brooke's voice represents no more than a repressed sex drive, but when I read that passage in ninth-grade English class, I nodded in recognition. Whether or not I would become be a nun-bride of music, I hoped to sound as deeply as I felt. In the same year I attended a confirmation class at the Methodist church, which culminated in a procession to the altar where we teenagers were supposed to kneel and repeat silently: "I place nothing higher than you, O Lord." Rolling my clasped hands over the polished brass altar rail, I found myself murmuring, "I place nothing higher than you, O Lord—except for Music." How not-guilty I felt for tailoring this rite of passage to my own vision of heaven. Praying to a deity whose gloomy-eyed portrait leaked from a cheap prayer card was nothing compared to harnessing myself to a life force. I wept with happiness at this breakthrough, this freedom, the wide, undulating Ahhh of space before me.

Saying what you mean, singing it right takes a ridiculously long time. Oh, how we stumble. MBRGR. Mxyzptlk! When I was 19, in music school, and absorbing my mother's concern that I find a husband, I grew so frightened of my desire to perform great music on the clarinet that I talked myself into believing I should slink away into a do-good, domestically correct profession, give up all that space that I knew lay beyond. Who would know I'd wimped out? Who would fault me?

So I enrolled in Music Therapy 101 and took field trips to clinics and hospitals. I saw a class of mentally retarded women learn to tell time by singing a song about hours and turning the hands of a large wooden clock. I watched a drug-numbed teenager's eyes flicker to life as he listened to a tape recording of Debussy's *La Mer* through a headset. Then at mid-term, I visited a children's ward where a music therapist was working with a boy of five named Bobby. Bobby had been severely injured in a boating accident and among his many lost functions was speech. He produced no words, only sharp chunks of static, much like those I had heard Krysti Fischer utter twelve years before. The goal of this day's session, the therapist explained, was to get Bobby to make a vowel sound, and since Halloween was coming up, she had decided to go for "ooo" by teaching him a song about ghosts.

> *In the night so dark and still, with*
> *owls and pumpkins, witches, too*
> *Floats a ghost so white and scary*
> *Rising up and crying "Boo!"*

Accompanying herself on a toy xylophone, the therapist sang the song through for Bobby. Bobby paid little attention. His gnarled body was strapped into a wheelchair; his misshapen head was protected by a white plastic helmet. The only parts of Bobby capable of free movement were his eyes, and so his gaze shot around the room randomly, crazily, it seemed, to what end I could not tell.

"Listen again, Bobby," the therapist said, catching his glance, grasping his arm, and once more she touched her tiny wooden mallets to the xylophone's rainbow bars. Again she sang: loudly, emphasizing each word and coming down hard on BOO. Again Bobby looked in every other direction: toward the floor, the ceiling, the door, toward me.

The therapist showed no sign of frustration. "Let's try it real loud this time, Bobby," she said, pinging a high note for emphasis, and this time, Bobby seemed to hear her. He turned his face toward the therapist as she sang, and he smiled at the word "ghost"

> *. . . so white and scary*
> *Rising up and crying*

"Boh!" Bobby yelped. "Bah! Boh!" Grinning, her eyebrows

raised in encouragement, the therapist replayed the final phrase on the xylophone.

Rising up and crying . . .

Bobby wiggled in his seat, chafing at the belts that held him, dislocating the helmet that protected his delicate skull. Then he drew a monstrously healthy breath that rattled every nut and bolt of his constraints, made such a ruckus, in fact, that two attendants rushed forward to seize and brake and block his rolling wheelchair.

"Boo!" cried Bobby, shaking with delight. "Boo, Boo, *Booooooo!*"

After I switched my major to clarinet-playing, I studied hard and learned, for example, about artistic doubt, a state of asphyxiation so soft and sneaky its "b" is silent. I also learned about the seductions of vocation. The "call" can motivate, but it can also block the way to open space. One day I hope to improvise in limitless air. At the moment one accepts that freedom, say the world's wise men and women, the voice demands that illusions die and pride take a powder. Who are you, anyway? A person with an instrument others taught you to sound. You haven't been called. You aren't even special. You are just lucky, and so you sing.

❧ GREEN COVE ❧

1968–1995

In the fall of my senior year in high school, I started driving up to Green Cove Springs. I skipped classes to do this, and in the beginning I had no destination other than north, out of town, away from dreary Titusville with its concrete shopping center and cinder-block homes. Titusville called itself Florida's Gateway to the Galaxies, and we had moved there from Ft. Lauderdale in 1962, when I was eleven, so my father could launch a business selling insurance to the Space Center's growing flock of engineers. His clients' beneficiaries, my classmates, eagerly gobbled the advanced math and science courses I avoided, and except for Rhonda Binkley, who won Junior Miss because she used vibrato when she sang the theme from *The Sound of Music*, I was the only person in my class with much musical talent.

I had to clear three hurdles to get away with skipping, and managed two of them before I realized I was setting myself up to break rules. The first was covering missed schoolwork, which was easy, because I didn't have any. So deep was my passion for music, so sure was my goal to be a great clarinetist, that I had convinced the guidance counselor to let me demote myself from advanced classes to the regular kind. "I need to spend every free minute practicing," I explained to her, and after a mild protest,

Miss Connor, who had a master's degree in conducting, praised my ambition and filled out the necessary forms.

The second hurdle was figuring out how to leave campus alone in a car without being questioned. Racial integration smoothed the way. Titusville High, the white school, and Gibson High, the black school, had just combined, and being literally across the railroad tracks from each other, the two joined as one institution. Students with classes on both campuses regularly walked back and forth across the tracks. Because I worked as an assistant to the choral director, who'd been assigned the music room of the former black school, I often transported stacks of music from one campus to the other. The parking lot monitors got used to seeing me load up my father's spare car, a blue Ford Falcon, to make the hauls; what they didn't know was that the choral director had a free period during my work hour. He never knew if I showed up or not. Eventually, I started driving over the tracks, and away—toward the Indian River to watch the water birds, or into one of the orange groves, where I might snitch a piece of fruit before returning to school.

One day I decided skipping one period wasn't enough—I needed at least two—and I developed the art of making excuses, written and oral. If you missed more than one class at Titusville High, you had to bring a note from home stating that you were sick, or had a doctor's appointment. My mother had always written these, so I began forging notes from my father, whose hand no one knew. When I started skipping whole school days and afternoons as well, I had to explain to my parents why I wouldn't be home until five or six. That was easy. I was staying after school to practice my clarinet.

I didn't drive far at first, but I nearly always headed north on U.S. Highway 1, along the Atlantic Ocean. The northern beach towns, I discovered, were poor relations to Palm Beach, Fort Lauderdale, and Miami, plagued by land deals gone wrong, hotels not filled, lives changed for the worse. Instead of golden, coarse-grained sand, they had fine gray dirt. Instead of languorous coconut palms, they had scrub palmetto and wild, thigh-slicing grass. Northern beaches had no shells, no lifeguards, and no public showers. They were often deserted and melancholy, even when the sun was shining. The only town of any size along the 150-mile stretch between Titusville and the state line at Jacksonville was Daytona Beach, which, outside of spring break in March, contained nothing more than a handful of Indian River citrus shops, Manny's Alligator Zoo (one scabby alligator fenced inside a concrete ditch), and the ghosts of Henry Ford, Louis Chevrolet and Ransom Olds, who once raced their prototypes in the sand.

New Smyrna Beach, 30 miles north of Titusville and my favorite spot for writing hormone-inspired poetry on the sand in the rain, was settled in the mid-1700s by a Scottish physician named Andrew Turnbull who tried to create a Mediterranean colony by importing Greeks and Italians to labor on his plantation in exchange for plots of land. Turnbull's dream went bust, but evidence of it remained: the ruins of a sugar mill, and Turnbull's unfinished house. There was also an Indian burial mound nearby. I explored the sugar mill ruins several times, fingering the cracks in the stones, creeping through doorless doorways, but I wouldn't leave the Falcon to examine the burial mound. All I could see from my blue vinyl bench seat was a grassy hill, which I imagined to be stuffed with bones.

If I'd driven beyond New Smyrna and Daytona Beach, I

might have seen the Fountain of Youth at St. Augustine. But just north of Daytona, U.S. 1 turned inland, away from the ocean path, first crossing I-95 (which was under construction), then Florida 100, which I followed through the poor, tropical farming villages of Andalusia and San Mateo. About ten miles past San Mateo, I caught U.S. 17, which led me north along the St. John's River toward the small town of Green Cove Springs.

Driving alone on the highway made me feel grown up. I liked stopping at convenience stores, which were new then, pulling out the wad of fives and ones I'd earned playing weekend gigs in the SilverTones Youth Big Band, and ordering a cherry Slurpee from the cashier, always a middle-aged woman named Edna or Doris who smoked Luckies and ratted her hair. I left each store quickly, chin first as if late for an appointment, biting back the lemony aftertaste of the Slurpee. Sometimes I stopped to buy a box of Kentucky Fried chicken, the breaded skin thick as carpeting and stinking of pepper and fat. I'd spread the white paper napkins with Colonel Sanders' twisted red face over my lap, hit the accelerator, and push out onto the highway, my hand in the chicken box. I loved my own silence, which I broke occasionally by singing old Girl Scout songs at the tops of my lungs.

Along the St. John's River, Spanish moss drifted like smoke from grandfather oaks, glass-insulated telephone lines, the roofs of shanties and aluminum trailers. Small farms and fishing camps seemed to be sliding into the water. No outsider had invested any fortunes here, no native ever dreamed of making one. Seminole Indians once lived along the river, taking in runaway slaves from Georgia and South Carolina, and I was as likely to see a black farmer as a white one, plowing earth his family had squatted on several generations before. I passed fresh-laundered work shirts pinned to white string lines swinging in the breeze, women in cotton dresses chasing tiny, biscuit-brown children who wore nothing but muddy underpants. The St. John's was the lower right-hand corner of the deep south, a pocket of dank green beauty, and I, a transplant bored by the air-brushed Space Center and its aliens, craved the certain history of the pot-holed roads, the rusted-out signs and the country gas pumps, where I sometimes used the Gulf credit card my father had given to me for emergencies.

It took me a couple of months to risk following the St. John's all the way to Green Cove Springs, because it was a two-hour drive each way, a full day's outing requiring complicated excuses and lots of snacks, and the result of being caught would be, I imagined, grim; my father had once revoked my library privileges for six months after I kept a book three weeks past the return date. His daughter needed to learn responsibility, he told the librarian. But one morning I didn't care about consequences, and I cranked up the Falcon and drove forever. By noon, I'd rolled into Green Cove, fewer than fifty miles from the Georgia line.

I knew someone in Green Cove Springs. His name was Spence and he played the clarinet, too; I had met him the year before in the All-State band. Spence was fat, redheaded, and excitable. He'd stared at me obsessively during the first rehearsal, puffing his cheeks and crossing his eyes, trying to make me laugh. I don't know why he picked me to entertain, to crack up. I believed I looked serious and attentive and beyond such childishness, and maybe that was the point. Spence hit pay dirt, and after that I was the one passing notes and initiating fake coughing fits.

A few weeks later, I bumped into Spence again at a solo-playing contest. He was chattering to anyone who would listen about a competitive music camp in North Carolina he planned to attend, and he insisted I go, too, for the sake of my brilliant career, so I applied for a scholarship and went that summer. It was my first time to travel out of Florida alone, to learn from professional musicians and perform with students who loved music as much as I did. Many nights I lay wide awake, ecstatic in my bunk bed, floating in the sweet, warm breath of an orchestra I'd heard hours before.

Spence embarrassed me at the camp—his stupid jokes and comic honks on the clarinet didn't seem so funny around serious musicians. Even so, I was grateful for his encouragement, and for the bottle of sparkling cider—which he believed to be champagne—he stole for my seventeenth birthday. Spence and the concerts and the gauze-ringed mountains of North Carolina convinced me that I was, indeed, born to music.

Dreams lie within for long periods of time, feeding on parts of you and fertilizing others, gestating this way and that, and sometimes you can mistake the baby's kick for the true thing, the whole child. Soon after my father graduated from high school, he left his family's farm in Indiana to strike out on his own. He was the only one of five children who did not settle near McCutchanville, and because he died soon after my Green Cove jaunts, I imagined for a long time that my furtive travels resembled his. I had been a chip off the old block, moving out into the world toward my heart's desire. I wouldn't know for forty years how wrong I was. At a family reunion in 2006, a cousin finally revealed that as youths, my father and hers had been singled out by our grandfather and beaten for small infractions, like dropping a forkful of hay. When he came of age, my father sprang free and kept moving for nearly two decades, including the Depression, working odd jobs and gambling and never calling home.

On the day I finally drove all the way to Green Cove Springs, I stopped at a pay phone and called the Clay County High School band room, where Spence spent the afternoons practicing and coaching younger students. I dropped my dime five times before working it into the slot. A girl with the voice of a small child whined hello. I could hear Spence in the background, yelling at someone to force more air through a saxophone, then yelling at the whiney girl for interrupting him. When he heard my voice, he screamed. I met him at the band room, and he paraded me around, announcing to everyone that I was even more talented than he was. The kids seemed much younger than my Titusville classmates. The boys' haircuts were uneven and some of the girls had dirty ankles. I sped the 125 miles home in time for dinner.

I drove to Green Cove Springs several times. Once, I listened to some of Spence's younger protégés rehearse solos and helped them with difficult passages, as he lacked the patience. Another time, I met Spence at St. Augustine Beach where we drank cokes, talked about clarinet reeds, and made fun of people we'd met at contests: the acne-gouged flute prodigy from Orlando who planned to forsake his musical gift and major in chemistry, the Tampa college band director's promiscuous daughter who always wore a matching dress, coat, and shoes.

Spence and I didn't last long. One week he finally declared his passion for me; the next week he announced he couldn't give me what I needed, whatever that meant. I'd wanted both proclamations, actually, and was relieved when they erupted back to back. I was beginning to feel nervous at home, and confused. The Falcon's muffler had fallen off. I couldn't explain how or where. I was preparing a concerto for a contest, the first solo I'd attempted with a piano accompaniment too difficult for my mother to pound out. Miss Connor, the guidance counselor, was calling me in for conferences because through some fluke of guesswork I had placed among the school's top ten scorers on the Florida twelfth grade test. I remember attending a meeting with the other nine, all straight-A students in chemistry and calculus, courses I had never taken, and hearing the principal, Mr. Everhart, say we were the leaders of tomorrow. I remember Mr. Everhart leafing through our school records then, and commenting, in front of everyone, that he didn't understand why I was there.

I returned to Green Cove Springs twice more; the first time was for senior prom. I'd been invited by one of Spence's classmates, Leland, a sensitive, green-eyed French Horn player who'd been raised Southern Baptist and aspired to a Catholic priesthood. Leland collected postcards of Renaissance paintings and owned a large black umbrella with a wooden handle. Just as I loathed Titusville, he couldn't wait to get away from small-time Green Cove; together we dreamed of dazzling futures in sophisticated society, even as we declared our admiration for the poetry of Rod McKuen. At the Clay County High prom, held in an old plantation house, Leland gave me a pale yellow orchid and kissed me beneath the moon in a pasture of warm cows. Leland and I are still friends. Today, he is the rector of an Episcopal church, a splendid inner-city cathedral in Baltimore. From time to time, he has fantasized about moving even farther from Green Cove, to Canada. But I don't think he will, because his calling is right where he is.

It is easy to confuse a place with a destination when it is your own strange ride you are aching for. Twenty-six years after the prom, I returned to Green Cove for the second time. I had flown from my home in Texas to south Florida for business, and at the end of the week, I drove north in a rented car along the Atlantic coast, windows down, gathering the salt air and the whoosh of the ocean. My musical career had stalled and my second marriage was coming apart; maybe, amid the familiar sights of my youthful trips, I would envision happiness to come. Maybe I would even move back to Florida! Midway, I stopped in New Smyrna for gasoline, and when I handed the attendant my credit card, I suddenly realized that my father had known all along about my high school junkets, from his Gulf Oil statements. And had never, bless him, said a word.

The road to Green Cove had changed, but not much. Moss and kudzu still swaddled the towns of Mims and Scottsmoor and Oak Hill, and Manny's Alligator Zoo was miraculously still in business, exhibiting the same bored reptile. Andrew Turnbull's sugar mill was open to visitors, and the Indian burial mound was intact, although a new sign bearing the Seal of the Great State of Florida indicated the true gravesite was only "thought to be in this area." Andalusia and San Mateo had double-wides instead of shacks; U.S. 17 along the St. John's River remained lush and beautiful. Green Cove Springs had changed, however. Commuters from Jacksonville had pushed down into it, spawning car dealerships and fast-food restaurants that crowded the view of the river. I drove around for an hour and couldn't find Clay County High School. Leland's creek-side home, a tan trailer adjacent to an old stone carriage house, had vanished, and the vacant lot was up for sale. I rolled in on the old driveway, got out, and looked around. The sun was bright, and I could still hear the mockingbirds over the road noise. I pulled a long hank of Spanish moss from the limb of an oak and stowed it in my skirt pocket. Then I walked over to a pay phone outside the new McDonald's and called Leland in Baltimore. The church secretary said he was meeting with the education committee.

"I'll be glad to get him for you," she said. "I'm sure he won't mind."

"Don't interrupt him," I said. "Tell him I was in Green Cove. I am calling from the road."

❧ HOW I GOT MY SOUTHERN ACCENT ❧

1974–1977

The Carriage Shop sat at the end of an Eisenhower-era shopping strip on North Monroe Avenue, just up from downtown Tallahassee, where the state capital's landscaping ran out. I had passed it riding the city bus from campus to the new mall to buy canned tuna and toilet paper, regarded the shop's wide bay window with the rod-jawed, tulle-wrapped mannequin posing in a black carriage and thought, "Old Lady Store." Now I'd been invited to interview there for a job as a clerk. Of course, I had nothing to wear.

I had two choices: call my mother long-distance for permission to buy another polyester dress with her Penney's charge card, or find something on sale elsewhere. It was 1974. Penney's wouldn't cut it. All-cotton, that holy sheeting of pure plant fibers requiring the martyrdom of ironing, had just been canonized in *Mademoiselle,* and I wanted to be as high-principled as the next girl. I went to a hole-in-the-wall that sold incense and love beads and T-shirts with satin ice cream cones and tongues stitched onto them, and bought a marked-down, flowered kettlecloth dress with a Chinese collar and rick-rack trim. I loved that dress. It made me feel like the free spirit

I was dying to be. But the next morning, in the plush, tailored company of Mizz Inez and Mizz Mary Eleanor, it hung on me like a gardening smock.

Mizz Inez and Mizz Mary Eleanor, the Carriage Shop's proprietors, were respectably hitched to misters, although Mizz Inez had the lean limbs, erect posture and steel-cut hair of an old-fashioned dean of women. She and Mizz Mary Eleanor, a plump matron with pocked, powdered cheeks and a gray flip frozen to her head, had been sorority sisters when Florida State was still an all-girl academy. They had majored in home economics and married nice young men who became lawyers. Mizz Inez and Mizz Mary Eleanor were also natives of Tallahassee, which had a lot to do with the success of their shop. In those days, loyalty to home blood transcended the advantages of discount shopping, even among Depression-generation Scarlett O'Haras who still held out for reduced-price carrots.

Mizz Inez, the stern one, interviewed me, which was unfortunate, because I intended to deliver a couple of lies. A shop-owner who traded on ancient allegiances would expect me to sign on for a decade, minimum, but as a musician, I considered any job with regular hours to be an annoying, and always temporary, ordeal. The truth was, I had just completed a degree in clarinet-playing at Florida State University and won a generous scholarship for graduate work at the New England Conservatory. But my boyfriend Ted, a Georgia-born pianist one year behind me, had lately hinted that his mother, a card-carrying member of the United Daughters of the Confederacy, disapproved of his intention to marry a Yankee after graduate school. "I can just tell she's had affairs," she'd told her only child, who dutifully reported back to me, oblivious to the weight of that comment. Using the high cost of living in Boston as the reason, I decided to delay my studies for one year to work, save, and ensure the wedding I thought I wanted.

Though I had worked on my stage presence for years, Mizz Inez's direct stare and high, twitching cheekbones nearly threw me off my game. Still, I managed to maintain the agreeable aura of an earnest inferior, even as I compared my limp hem to her creamy knit skirt. Was I finished with school? Yes. Did I plan to settle down in Tallahassee? Yes. Did I think I would fit in at the Carriage Shop? Oh, yes.

I tried riding the bus to work the first day, but it dropped me in front of the Carriage Shop at 8:35 instead of 8:30, and Mizz Inez pinned me so with her gray eyes that the next morning I got up an hour earlier, bolstered my calves with reinforced pantyhose, and trudged the three miles from my campus apartment, to be on time. Ted, a straight-A student whose own wardrobe consisted of black pants and white shirts, admired my desire to be punctual and often walked me to work. Mizz Inez and Mizz Mary Eleanor thought this was sweet, and when my consort introduced himself one day and they heard a red-clay accent they could trust, I knew I could take the bus occasionally and get away with it.

Despite its fine reputation among Southern women of a certain age, The Carriage Shop was no gilt-trimmed parlor perfumed to titillate failing olfactory nerves, but a dimly-lit room with beige walls, plain, clean carpeting, and modest means for display. A glass showcase to the right held beaded evening bags, white gloves, and "quality" costume jewelry. Behind it, smart leather pocketbooks climbed the wall on two ranks of wooden shelves, staggered like steps of a pyramid. Next to them, a series of framed cubbyholes contained folded sweaters, blouses, and clear plastic boxes of lacy panties, bras, slips and camisoles. The walnut desk, where we wrote up the tickets and wrapped gifts in green paper embossed with pink strawberries, stood adjacent to the cubbyholes. Behind the desk along both walls, dresses hung quietly in long recessed racks that reminded me of bedroom closets with the doors taken off. In the center of the store, free of all demure encasement, stood the sale rack.

    The Carriage Shop also had plenty of mirrors: a pedestalled oval on the jewelry counter, a wide beveled pane set just beneath the peak of the climbing purses, and a plain, full-length swath next to the desk. In the back near the door to the three curtained dressing rooms stood an antique table with a gold gesso mirror and a pink brocade couch where customers could rest, and where we clerks were discouraged from sitting. Customers or no, we were expected to keep busy: refolding the sweaters, spacing the dress hangers, propping up the handbags.

    Patsy, the senior clerk, was a pretty, middle-aged woman, mother of college students, wife of an engineer. She had wide hips wrapped in rosy floral skirts and a high voice that sounded like it was trapped inside a picnic basket, and because she'd recently strained her back planting a camellia she was allowed, on slow mornings, to sit on the couch and knit. Jan, an ex-cheerleader with teenaged daughters and an accountant at home, teased her short blonde hair to such transparent heights you could read a copy of Modern Bride through it. Jan had taught second grade in Alabama but wasn't certified in Florida, so she, like Patsy, worked twenty hours a week at The Carriage Shop, spending her wages on Quiana shirtwaists and waiting for something else to do. That left the two full-timers: me, and Rosalie, a round black woman who wore a starched gray uniform with a white apron.

Rosalie unpacked the dress boxes in the stockroom, steamed and hung the new outfits, and polished the glass display case, over and over. Rosalie made the Carriage Shop customers feel at home. Some of them still lived in plantation houses near Thomasville, Georgia, twenty miles north, just over the state line.

I had lived in Florida since the age of five, when my mother and father, who hailed from Maine and Indiana, moved our family down from Maryland. But they settled us just north of Miami, and I had never encountered pure southern talk until I joined the ladies at the Carriage Shop. Ted's voice, steamed nearly to pudding in his small hometown southeast of Atlanta, daily undulated in my ear, but I was in love with his straight heart and strict work habits and only heard our differences when his mother was around. At the Carriage Shop, everyone ya-alled and how doo-ed you to death, and by the end of my first day there, every sentence I uttered sounded like scrap lumber falling off a truck.

I didn't actually wait on anyone until the end of the first week, although each hankie-holding matron who tottered in had to size me up. ("You the new girl? Well, *isn't* that nice!") Most of the customers were regulars fawned upon by Jan and Patsy; a few requested Mizz Inez or Mizz Mary Eleanor, to demonstrate how far back their accounts went. I felt as if I had been dropped off at a cotillion ball with no date, so I spent my time folding and re-folding the silk slips and camisoles, trying to catch Rosalie's downcast eye as she polished the accessory counter to ether.

Finally, I made my debut. Mizz Inez and Mizz Mary Eleanor were at lunch, Jan was off, and Patsy had three rows to go on a mohair sleeve.

My customer was young, not yet thirty, and I thought perhaps she had made a mistake choosing the Carriage Shop, despite the fact that she wore a well-cut pantsuit and carried a Coach handbag. I approached her shyly in my kettlecloth, but as soon as I offered a two-syllable Hello, she averted her eyes and skimmed over to the size 6s. "Ah'm looking for the new Joneses," she called back over her shoulder. "Mary Eleanor left word with my maid."

The young woman's claim to rank worked on me instantly. I jumped back behind the sale rack and scanned the shop for Patsy, who was pulling herself up from the couch. "Hel-loh-oh, Mizz Gilbert," Patsy said. "We had three boxes of Jones New York come in and they're all out on the floor. The beige two-piece would look div-ahn on you."

I took the cue, spotted the smart beige ensemble, and carefully extricated it from the dour McMullen knits and the knife-pleated Tanners. Tightening my lips, I held it up for Mrs. Gilbert to admire.

"Mary Eleanor is always right," Mrs. Gilbert said. "It's div-ahn. Wrap it for me, puh-lease."

I knew some customers preferred to try the clothes at home instead of being waited on in a dressing room. I had watched Ted's mother do this—choose two or three dresses from her own version of The Carriage Shop and try them later in the privacy of her bedroom. There was a difference, though: The Carriage Shop customers kept what they took, calling in the charge, while my future mother-in-law, a retired children's librarian whose family, she often reminded me, "lost everything" in "The War" (the one between the states), always returned her selections. Having taken part in the most public part of the ritual, the privilege of taking without paying, she denied herself the quiet pleasure of purchase, even though she and her husband, a postmaster, had done quite well for themselves—far better than my parents, who led riskier professional lives and splurged on road trips. "Ah just can't see spending the money," she'd say.

As I swaddled the new Jones in white tissue paper, Mrs. Gilbert flipped through the sale rack. "Ah really should consider these," she said, with a little moan. "Jim says the bills are getting out of hand."

"Sometimes it's hard to keep track," I said, trying to sound conspiratorial. Mrs. Gilbert picked up the pink Carriage Shop sack by its wicket handles and left.

It didn't take me long to despise every piece of clothing I owned, down to the underwear. Even my bras were cheap—Playtexes, not Olgas. But at $2.25 an hour, I couldn't afford to replace my entire wardrobe, so I began to plot my way to just one Carriage Shop-quality outfit. The only clothes in the shop that I actually liked were the Joneses—Mrs. Gilbert's label. But even though I was entitled to a thirty per cent employee discount, I couldn't touch them. The fifty per-cent off rack was a stretch for me. One day, however, a navy blue Jones skirt, size ten, got marked down thirty per cent, and because I'd been made keeper of the sale rack, I jammed the skirt in among the fourteens so no ten would find it. Two weeks later Mizz Inez cut the price to fifty per cent and hung the skirt back in its proper place. I bought it and wore it to work the next day. But the shabby white blouse I paired it with pulled the beautiful skirt down a few income brackets, so I chose a suitable sale blouse, stuffed it in with the sixteens, and waited. By the end of the month, my new outfit was complete.

My resourcefulness delighted Ted, who was saving $25 a month from his church pianist's job to purchase a modest engagement ring. As aspiring musicians we imagined a fulfilling life of sacrifice, poor cuts of beef in exchange for the Bach Gesellschaft. That year I happened to be overdosing on Tchaikovsky's opera *Eugen Onegin,* a tragedy of unrequited love submerged in cloying, hypersensitive harmonies. Ted was analyzing the early symphonies of Ludwig Spohr with a No. 2 pencil.

Properly attired, I threw myself into my sales work, offering my services with confidence, as one expensive dresser to another. Instead of hanging back, I strode around The Carriage Shop like a former Cotton Queen, matching scarves to belts and bags to beads, exclaiming, "Whah yez, Mizz Beauregard, a Peter Pan collar's always in stahl!" And then one day a south Georgia matron mistook me for her daughter's sorority sister, and I heard myself gush meaninglessly, "Whah, Ah'm so-oh sorry, and how nah-ahce of yee-ew!"

Losing your tongue is a major achievement. For months, without thinking, I'd imitated what I heard, letting my lips go soft, working my jaw just enough to push out the soggy diphthongs. Ted's mother came to town at the height of it, seemed impressed by the Carriage Shop, but still not with me. We drove her around in her '52 Plymouth, took her to McClay Gardens to see the azaleas, to Morrison's Cafeteria for lunch, to the FSU library to see dedicated young people studying. Everywhere, she saw things she did not like: women without bras, men without underpants. "The bottom rail is on the top," she declared fifty-thousand times, her son nodding vigorously in agreement. The week after she left, I spent three hours waiting hand and foot on a sour old belle from Thomasville whose son was getting married—engineered, in fact, four stunning Southern Lady outfits, complete with stockings, purses and earrings to match. "Yo-ah son wi' be so prou-oud!" I kept repeating, pulling my own string.

In the spring, Ted and I agreed to audition for two graduate schools and attend the one that accepted us both. I placed third at the Yale clarinet audition, but there were only two openings for the instrument that year. My Georgia sweetheart, who now intended to be a scholar, made it in.

"So we'll go to Michigan!" I said, waving our letters from Ann Arbor.

"I guess so," Ted said.

Around that time a new customer wandered into the Carriage Shop. She was a plain woman of about forty, no make-up, wearing a loose cotton shift and a pair of Swedish clogs. Her legs were bare—I could see the rough skin of her heels—and she carried a denim shoulder bag. It was a slow day and I was on my own, so I watched quietly for a few minutes while the woman regarded the carriage mannequin by the door. The mannequin leaned forward slightly, straight as an ironing board, legs crossed, her left hand extended, palm up, beckoning. The long middle finger of that hand was broken, inadvertently bound with masking tape into a rude gesture. I was the only employee in The Carriage Shop who found that funny. The plain woman moved in close to get a good look at the finger. She laughed out loud, turned with an easy flourish, and headed for the sale rack.

The woman seemed familiar but I couldn't place her. I

stepped out from behind the pink brocade sofa and drawled my greeting.

"No help—just looking," she said, her accent flat as Kansas. She thunked her denim bag on the floor and began whipping through the marked-down clothes, starting with the 6s, working all the way to the eighteens, where she found a certain size 10 bathrobe, half off. She tried it on over her dress, right in the middle of the store.

"I'll take this," she said.

As the woman handed me her check I realized who she was: the wife of Ted's piano professor, a well-known pianist herself who gave concerts occasionally on campus. I had seen her once before, but seated onstage in a beaded dress, summoning Mozart from a Steinway grand. She was, I understood only subconsciously then, a woman who knew the difference between pretension and stagecraft. I watched her make a quick study of the rest of the shop as I wrote up her ticket, and when I handed over her purchase, she offered a charitable smile. She wouldn't be back.

In May, Ted withdrew the $200 in his savings account and bought me a diamond solitaire—modest, but of high quality. Then he told me he had written a last-minute letter of intent to Yale.

"I couldn't help it," he said. "It would kill Mother if I didn't go. It's *Yale!* Don't you understand?"

"I guess so," I said.

My last three months at the Carriage Shop went slow as

the Suwannee River. I grew careless all around. My trophy Jones skirt was too hot for summer, and when we got in a cute new line of flowered cotton skirts and jackets, I bought similar fabric at Cloth World, copied the outfits at a fraction of the cost using the sewing machine my mother bought me for graduation, and wore them to work, drawing glares from Mizz Inez. I stopped spending my lunch hour trying on hostess gowns and hunkered down in the stock room eating cheap, stinky chicken livers from Colonel Sanders across the street, and pondering a stack of books I'd begun to read before falling in love with a Southern Baptist.

One day, Mizz Mary Eleanor discovered me hiding among the new Diane von Furstenburgs, underlining key passages in *A Psychoanalytic Study of Jesus*. "Now why would anybody want to read a book like that?" she said.

I broke the news to Mizz Inez: I'd decided to go back to school. She narrowed her eyes as if she'd known it all along and wrote me a bonus check: $10 for every month I'd worked. It didn't help much. In just short of a year at the Carriage Shop, I'd managed to support myself with no help from my parents, but not to save. I was going to Michigan as I might have gone to Boston: penniless, sans fiancé, and leaving my first full-time employer in the lurch. Jan was leaving, too, to study for her Florida teaching certificate, and Patsy's back had finally given out completely. That left Rosalie, who, I had decided after countless attempts at simple exchange, may have been oppressed but was also pretty well matched to her job. I spent the month of August at the sewing machine, running up wool pantsuits for my first northern winter in eighteen years, and when I showed up in Ann Arbor looking like J.C. Penney's fall catalogue, my major professor sighed deeply and said, "Well, well. It's been a long time since I taught a young lady from the South."

The next day I chucked the pantsuits, walked down to State Street with my Carriage Shop bonus and bought three pairs of Levis, a down jacket, and a book by Paul Tillich called *The Courage to Be*. Within a month, I reclaimed my long I's and A's, and in a brief spell of over-correction, eliminated all contractions, plus words like "lovely," "wonderful" and "divine." Thirty years later, "divine" is still off-limits, not that I'm ever compelled to use it.

In the two years that followed, fate delivered a tragedy, and then a choice. During my first semester at Michigan, both of my parents were killed in a car accident, and although Ted flew down to Florida for the funeral, I bore the weight of my grief alone, in a new environment. Then, eight months after my parents were buried in Indiana, Ted broke our engagement with a Dear Jane letter. His mother, still clinging to her dream of a Southern daughter-in-law, had convinced him that his father, the survivor of two heart attacks, would surely bolt heavenward on a third if their son married me. I was in New Hampshire then, taking a break from music and studying Frost and Melville on the shores of Lake Winnepesaukee with twenty other Michigan students. After the shock of my fiancé's betrayal had softened to relief in the local pubs, I began planning to begin adult life alone in Boston. Just then, Ted phoned, begging me to help him slash the apron strings. I was too freshly orphaned to say no.

As our brief marriage commenced, Ted accepted a teaching position in New Orleans and I, still able to masquerade as a southerner, won a solo gig conducting tours of a historic home in the French Quarter. By then I'd gotten wise to the ways a musical ear and the desire to be accepted can fork a woman's tongue, and instead of trying to fit in, I played with my gift for switching accents. "Where did you grow up?" bus-pale tourists from upstate New York and Ohio and would ask, and I might answer "South Florida," "Georgia," "Michigan" or even "Indiana," "Maine."

One spring day during my lunch hour, loitering comfortably among the itinerant street artists on Jackson Square, I admitted to myself that I wouldn't last any longer at tour guiding than I had at Southern ready-to-wear. Could it be so, I wondered, gazing up at a flock of migrating sparrows that trilled and flittered over the stone general, could it be true that I have flung my voice into the wrong livelihood, or the wrong life?

❦ CIRCULAR BREATHING ❦
for Mary
with gratitude to j.s.

1961–1996

I

When I was ten, my mother told me I was the middle child, not the oldest. My mother also mentioned a miscarriage, a boy who would have been named Douglas, but it was my sister Haverill who gurgled and sucked and cried for eight long months, and whose small body lies beneath a gray stone next to my mother's parents near Bangor, Maine.

The fact of a sister who died before I was born was first fascinating, then scary, as if a meteor I'd imagined in a toy telescope was suddenly reported to be real, and heading my way. I do not know where the unusual and elegant name Haverill came from, but, my mother explained later, the little girl was a source of embarrassment for my grandmother Bond, not because she bore a name with no provenance, but because she arrived nine months to the day after my parents eloped half way across the country, in Indianapolis. My mother, whose first name was Helen, told me that on the afternoon of Haverill's birth in Bangor, Grandmother tore into the hospital room, sensible shoes a-pounding, demanding to be told again exactly what day in February, 1943 her 26 year-old daughter had married this 37 year-old man, a fellow recreation director in an Indiana Red Cross rehabilitation center, an Indiana native named George McCutchan.

No one told Grandmother Bond that my parents had known each other all of two months before their wedding. The story goes that one day, as my father was leading a group of wounded, recovering soldiers in a light round of basketball, a Red Cross official appeared on the court and handed him an unexpected transfer to Germany. That evening after the staff supper, my father said to my mother, "Marry me now. We may never see each other again." Having in common good hearts, high spirits, and histories as high school basketball stars, they signed up for a five-minute ceremony at the Indianapolis courthouse with two Red Cross colleagues as witnesses. Haverill was conceived a few hours later. My father's transfer to Germany was canceled.

Haverill resembled stocky, dark-eyed George, not fair, blue-eyed Helen. Both of my parents had dark brown hair, but Haverill's was nearly red. ("Auburn," my mother said. "We don't know where it came from.") She was born with defective kidneys and died the following spring at Boston Children's Hospital. Douglas's miscarriage occurred three or four years later, and finally, seven years after my parents' impulsive wartime union, my mother carried a healthy child to term in Washington, DC with the help of diethylstilbestrol, a miscarriage prevention drug later proven to cause infertility in female offspring. I remember very clearly the day in 1989 when, after years of tests and surgeries and obscure diets, I was invited, because of my history and proximity to the age of forty, to participate in an assisted fertilization program at a hospital in Austin, Texas, where I live.

Part of my admission ticket was the letter my parents had received from Boston Children's Hospital in 1944, acknowledging the cause of Haverill's death—a detail that somehow contributed to my doctor's opinion that without extraordinary aid, I was in danger of ending my line.

I wasn't raised as a first-born, but as something slightly different: the too-long-awaited child, the one that finally took, God Bless Her, she's got to be a winner. I did not feel the full weight of this until I was thirteen or fourteen, when, with my mother's unflagging support on the piano I began to work seriously toward a future as a clarinetist. Perhaps the risk of a musical vocation along with dreams of an untraditional life away from the small central Florida town where we lived then agitated me as much as the pressure of fulfilling someone else's expectations.

Anyway, I sensed that there was something I was supposed to take care of because no one else was going to do it, and I ached for relief from whatever that was. My sister, Mary Estalene (named for an aunt who died of tuberculosis at 16), born two years after me, could not help. We shared our father's wry sense of humor, which saved us from many a rivalrous argument, but she was less daring than I, frequently ill with asthma, and, it seemed to me, overly sheltered for it. What I really needed at that age was a mentor who understood both my ardor for art as well as my more conventional desire to succumb to passionate sex in a guilt-free coma.

My mother openly understood the art part and threw much of her energy into finding me decent clarinet teachers, challenging music to learn and rare bits of culture, like the London Symphony's winter concerts in Daytona Beach, where

I first heard the rich, molasses tone of a professional clarinetist. I left my mother behind guiltily when I advanced to sonatas and concertos with accompaniments too difficult for her to play, yet she continued to monitor my social life, chaperoning high school band trips, much to my displeasure, and encouraging me to join the sorts of school clubs I abhorred but which she had enjoyed as a student. Her 1939 University of Maine senior yearbook contains extensive proof that she belonged to a sorority, a service club, a women's sports honor club and several women's athletic teams. Her major was psychology, and because she always spoke of her college years fondly, I, who read books late at night under the covers with a flashlight, imagined that she had been an exceptional student.

After her death I discovered her transcript in an old file folder, and it was loaded with C's. I realized then that my mother had been more of a jock than a scholar, saw why she once went so far as to ask a high-ranking citizen to sponsor me for a service organization all the popular girls in my high school belonged to. (I turned down the offer with a slam of my bedroom door; a few years later, I'd slam down the phone on college sororities.) But what mother who had spent ten happy years as a Girl Scout administrator and several more helping the public at the Titusville, Florida Chamber of Commerce wouldn't have done the same thing? She worked very hard for me. Yet, just as I mistakenly assumed she topped the Dean's List, my mother failed to see that I might best commune with and contribute to the world in less socially organized ways.

What my mother and I did share, the legacy I gratefully received from her, is a spirited curiosity about natural surroundings and the details close at hand. Her father had been a well-known Maine conservationist, a convivial hunter and fisherman who sold feed and seed to support his sharp-sighted wife and their three children. As his oldest child, and a tall, strong one, my mother learned to hike, canoe and camp vigorously, at an early age. When I was five and we moved from Washington, D.C. to the Atlantic coast of Florida, my mother wasted no time acquiring handbooks for shells, fish and water birds. Within weeks she and I could identify every shell on Ft. Lauderdale beach, brushing with our salty fingers the hardened lines of sand from mahogany turkey wings, opalescent pen shells and the tinkly, coin-like discs nicknamed "Baby's Feet" for the imprint left behind by the squishy animal.

Soon after that my mother proclaimed the sweltering, mosquito-infested Everglades an incomparably beautiful landscape and went off with a Girl Scout troop to camp there. She returned from the haunts of crocodiles and poisonous plants with a livid, weeping rash along one arm, shoulder to hand, and never complained, just kept slathering on pink Caladryl until it dried up. Today, her fearless attachment to the earth seems puzzling coupled with her circumspect approach to sex education—but then, New Englanders are full of contradictions. If, during my teen years, my mother feared I was working up to losing my innocence the minute I left home, which I was, she never acknowledged it. (I have only one memory of her involvement with my pathetic love life, when late one night I stole into the kitchen to perform the ritual burning of an ex-boyfriend's picture. She tiptoed in, chuckled, and helped me wave the ashes of a loud-mouthed, redheaded clarinet player into the sink.) Though her own mother's sense of propriety irked her, she was still inclined to value appearances, smoothing over lust, discomfort, apprehension. I felt powerless to change this—my mother was, among many things, dignified, in a way that was entirely natural, not posed, and I depended on that dignity for a certain measure of confidence in myself.

I tend to agree with a British poet of my parents' generation, William Empson, who wrote: "Do not look to family for soul-mates. It makes for a kind of incest." Yet if I could turn back the clock, I would find the courage to demand a closer relationship with my father, with whom I suspect I shared a meditative streak. My father was raised on a farm and taught early to cut wheat and butcher hogs, yet he kept a notebook of poems he had written, and which I did not discover until after he died. All of his poems plod toward predictable rhymes—they are modeled on the sorts of verses he might have memorized in the one-room Indiana school he attended with his two brothers and three sisters. The summer he was 17, he left home to work at Yellowstone National Park as a waiter and after-dinner entertainer. His talent was reading poetry aloud. During his twenties and early thirties, which coincided with the Depression, he traveled all over the country, working as a hosiery salesman, a carnival roustabout, a bouncer in a pool hall.

When World War II broke out, he tried to enlist in each branch of the armed forces and was turned down repeatedly because of flat feet and a tuberculosis scar on one lung. By the time I was born, he had become a million-dollar salesman for the Equitable Life Assurance Society in Washington, D.C. and was soon to be promoted to a district managership in Ft. Lauderdale, Florida. When I was very young my father was good-natured and patient, always ready to read me a story, give me a ride on his shoulders, fix my favorite breakfast and his, soft-boiled eggs on toast. But as I reached adolescence he was more than sixty years old, struggling to float a new business in Titusville, a Space Center boomtown, while attempting to save for two daughters who were going to college, something he wished he could have done himself. Relatives say he would have majored in history; among the few books he had time to read when I was in my teens was a thick biography of John Quincy Adams, and he was politically involved to the extent that he occasionally donated to Republican election campaigns.

My father possessed a strong native intelligence that could be read in his eyes, and it often presented itself in astute judgments of human character and the ability to explain anything to anyone smoothly and logically. One summer when I was ten or eleven he very calmly and methodically taught me to play tennis, which he and my mother had played together at a Washington, D.C. country club early in their marriage. Each time I waved my racket at empty air, he said, "You're standing too close to the net. Stand back, watch carefully, and move to *meet* the ball." I remember thinking how that advice could be applied in other situations, and I believe it crystallized his approach to living.

In those days, the only anxiety I ever saw in my father was linked to his fear of heights, a weakness divulged at the 1964 World's Fair in New York when he declined a 120-foot elevator ride to the top of Port Authority's heliport. Ascending to our airy view of Flushing Meadow, Mom whispered to Mary and me that Dad had long ago suffered a traumatic fall in a silo. Later I would learn of his financial worries, but he kept the details between himself and my mother, as would many parents attempting to give their children a smooth start. The heat of those worries nevertheless revealed itself in uncommon but cruel physical outbursts: slaps of his belt for talking back, and once in my late teens, the beating of our dog Jonas, who on a clear summer night would not stop barking at the moon. I have forgiven my father for his strikes at me because he grew up in a family that used belts on older children and there is no question that I, angry that so much went unsaid, provoked him. But I have not quite forgiven him for his mistreatment of Jonas, and I wish I might fully understand the temporary quirk or compulsion that made him turn an innocent animal into one that bit.

Despite their most human shortcomings, my parents were intelligent, honest people who encouraged creative pursuits and never insisted I feign devotion to subjects I cared nothing about. They had no use for bravado of any kind, complained of little, volunteered at church, were sought by their friends and acquaintances as advisors and confidantes. And because in their own ways they left empty the space for the person I was trying to become, I found it necessary and natural to make up an alter ego, Lydia, named after the beautiful heroine of Kenneth Roberts' novel. I was twelve when I did that, and over the next several years, when I had questions, problems or outrageous dreams I couldn't share with my mother or father, I wrote secret letters to her. Then I took up Lydia's pen and wrote thoughtful, big sister responses.

II

The campus police notified me on November 2—All Soul's Day, I learned later, having been raised in Methodist churches, which observed few holidays outside Christmas and Easter. Now there would be a new holiday to observe, a day to remember, that November 2 and every one after that—the day in 1974 when an officer from the University of Michigan's security force rapped on the door of my dorm room, scaring me half out of my new blue robe, quilted, the kind you never needed in Florida, and asked was I who I was—yes—then call your aunt in Maine, immediately. Your parents have been in an accident.

Accident stands erect at the edge of a shelf, falls off, breaks. It is a given, it is a done deal. You taste the metal of inevitability, you hear the dull thump of something large, lost.

Your mother and father were on a trip. Take the next flight to Orlando. Your neighbors will meet you and take you to the hospital.

Hospital is pity so delicate you know you're in for heart-splitting news, biting astringents applied with the softest of cloths. My heart is not in my throat, it has jumped up into my jaws, which knock back and forth on clay hinges as I sleepwalk through the act of asking a friend, Can you take me, Detroit Metro, a flight at eleven, I'll pack fast.

The long flight, the long stares out the window. Typically intense graduate music student, trying inexplicably to read Kierkegaard and checking her nose periodically for shine (it was something to do). The last time I saw my mother was two months before, when she drove me from my undergraduate apartment in Tallahassee to my graduate dorm in Ann Arbor. By then she knew I would survive without social clubs. She was happy for both of us. She kept her hotel room in the Michigan Union two days longer than planned (re-living her carefree days at the University of Maine, I imagined) and I, drunk on my escape from the south, couldn't wait for her to leave me alone. My father had already begun to fade for me because during my last year at Florida State he'd grown even quieter than usual, and unexplainably, maddeningly grumpy. In Michigan, my mother finally told me why—he had been suffering from prostate trouble and, having always been vigorously healthy, was frightened of surgery. He didn't think I needed to know about his problems.

I chew the airline chicken, try to make Kierkegaard relate to the moment. I nearly succeed. Or does the convoluted theology I barely understand merely keep my imagination on hold? I know nothing except Accident, and it will be hours before this word reveals the story behind it. And now it is dusk, the plane lands near orange trees, our next-door neighbors greet me at the gate, tell me we are going straight to the hospital near the Kennedy Space Center, the "Gateway to the Galaxies." The accident happened yesterday, Bertie and Bill whisper. Your folks were on their way to see friends in Tampa. I nod, too frightened to press for details. I ask only if the hospital has good doctors. "They are receiving excellent care," Bertie says. I pick at my cuticles, hiding my hands in the well of my skirt. Bill asks me about school and I force some meaningless sentences about my impatience with Heinrich Schenker's theory of harmony. The drive takes 45 minutes. It is 80 degrees out, and I shiver the whole way.

Bertie guides me down the green corridor. Let's stop by the chapel first, she says, and I suspect nothing more than a moment of prayer, for Bertie would do that, but we step inside and I am in the midst of what, in any other room, would appear to be a birthday surprise party, but it is not, it is a crowd of people, some I do not recognize, all from Titusville First Methodist, all waiting to surround me, and they do, as Mary moves from their midst to tell me, Oh, Ann, Dad went four hours ago.

My mother is completely, strikingly white. She is nearly six feet long, commands her intensive care bed as once, with her poised and confident stride, she commanded the eyes of strangers in a room. Now I am a stranger, gazing in shock at her thoroughly blanketed form, none of her flesh showing except for the pale skin of her face below the skull, taped soundly like a cut thumb. The nurse tells me the surgeon shaved her rich black and silver hair to drain fluid from her brain. Next to the bed, the square eye of a machine flickers red with my mother's serrated pulse. I feel the nurse watching for my reaction, preparing to catch me if I faint. My mother is completely white, she is sleeping, she is dreaming, she is wrapped in ancient, magical gauze and will rise up from the bed, shake off the tubes and wires, and float someplace where she will look down kindly and tell me that it is all right, it is a dream, I will wake up.

My mother and father set off for Tampa on a Friday afternoon. A few miles outside of town, near the access lanes for a throughway, a sixteen year-old boy driving a white Cadillac swung off the highway on a one-way ramp and entered the road my parents were on, one of those long, straight, two-lane paths slapped down on marshland so flat and unvaryingly gray with sawgrass you believe you're the only person for miles, particularly at dusk. The boy did not notice he was on a two-way road, and stayed on the left. My mother and father drove toward him in their little brown Dodge. My father had the wheel—he swerved sharply to the right shoulder. (Years later, I wonder: Was his prostate bothering him that day? Were his reflexes unusually slow?) My father's side took the grill of the Cadillac. The teen-aged driver suffered a broken arm.

Someone took Mary and me to see the Dodge because the insurance company wanted us to confirm that it was a loss. The Dodge was a crumpled soda can. Right then I began the periodic imaginings—what it felt like to be my father or my mother, driving along in that little car, suddenly realizing that what they saw in front of them was not the rear of another automobile, but the front of one. My mother would scream "Mac! Get over!" and grab the wheel. My father would mutter, "What the dickens—" and jerk the wheel hard to the right, leaning away from the blow of the Cadillac, into his wife.

We slept in our old bedrooms in the tiny tract house, awash in our parents' scents. Our bodies ached from an excess of sorrow, sobs that, with no warning, ruptured our chests. Here were our father's blue cotton pajamas, still hanging on the back of the bathroom door. His body, stopped just short of 68 years, was at the funeral home, waiting. Waiting for our mother's 57 year-old one, because, the surgeon said, she was holding on by a very fine thread, and we should wait a few days because—no one actually articulated this—one double funeral would be easier to orchestrate than two single ones. If our mother continued to live, she would never awaken. I prayed for her death.

One of my mother's two brothers, a biologist for the state of Maine, flew down to help us. I don't remember where Uncle Lyn stayed—in our house? At a neighbor's? In a motel?

My father's sisters and brothers, older people in their 70s, drove down in tandem from Indiana, straight through, stopping only to change drivers. Neighbors brought food. The minister visited daily. A boy with whom Mary and I had gone to high school dropped by several times, none of us knowing that three weeks later he would die suddenly of a brain tumor and I would plan the music for his funeral, as well.

There were useful things we could do to fill the time. We walked the funeral home showroom, rows of fancy metal trunks thrown open to display satin linings. All Mary and I could think to do was shop as our mother had taught us. Don't buy the cheapest—it will look tawdry and quickly fall apart. Don't buy the most expensive, either—pricey merchandise is over-rated, contains extras you don't need. Classic looks and good value lie somewhere in between. Something in me gravitated toward the simple varnished wood—our father would have preferred it—but mightn't that look disrespectful, or even cheap to a church congregation? I gestured toward the least gaudy of the mid-priced caskets, asked Mary what she thought. "Sure," she said. In most respectful tones, the funeral director informed us he had two in stock, should we require both.

Two days later, the surgeon phoned and said there were only a few hours left. Mary and Uncle Lyn and I drove over then, but we were too late. They had already turned off the machines. Mary stepped forward to touch one of our mother's blanketed feet. I hung back to watch and remember the scene.

The funeral director asks if we want visitation with open caskets. Mary and I are ambivalent; if we weren't surrounded by people who have been adults so much longer than we have, we would say it's not to our taste, we don't want it. But a relative reminds us that we haven't seen our father at all, not even in a hospital bed, and the funeral director insists our parents will look stunning. "Not a mark on your father," he says. "Your mother, because of the brain surgery, will require a wig."

So Mary and I go shopping at Wigs 'n Things in Miracle City Mall. It is a vast, mirrored store, forested with tall poles thick with hair, hundreds of wigs clinging to invisible wooden pegs. We tiptoe among them, patting crowns, fingering tendrils, searching for something that could belong to our mother. Desperate for release, I grab an outrageous platinum haystack, consider for a moment pulling it on hard over my ears. Mary eyes me, smiling, but we know it's too early for this.

Our father looks wonderful: as if, as they say, he is sleeping. He wears one of the business suits we chose from his closet. The black hairs on the backs of his hands curl slightly, as if blood is still plumping the skin. His repose calms me. His self-possession is upper class. Who would guess he was raised on a farm?

But our mother, in life the more sophisticated of the two, looks awful. The wig we finally chose is askew, and the funeral people have applied too much make-up, especially around her mouth, which drags down to one side from the head injuries. The bright red lipstick, which she would have hated, clashes with the purple paisley dress she used to wear to church. I am appalled, crushed, humiliated for my mother. I want to scream at the sniveling, opportunistic undertaker, grab my parents' bodies, race them out of the funeral home and do something normal, like buy them milkshakes and take them to the beach.

But running away is impossible. Relatives and townspeople are waiting for me to finish my viewing so they can get a better look at my parents and at the two daughters, ages 21 and 23 who, they say, nodding sagely, shaking their heads in disbelief, will carry on as well as their parents would expect them to. Besides, I'd go crazy with grief at the beach—those miles of gray sand, that infinite horizon.

A few days after our parents' funeral, Eastern Airlines called to inform Mary and me that they had accidentally dented one of the caskets changing planes en route to the family cemetery in McCutchanville, Indiana. Eastern would, as part of their award-winning customer service policy, replace the casket at no cost to us, and if an exact duplicate weren't available in Indiana, they would match it as closely as possible. Would this be acceptable to us in our hour of grief?

Mary and I had enough on our hands. Convinced by our Indiana relatives that we had participated in enough rituals, we had stayed behind to begin two more: clean out the house so we could put it up for rent (the sales market was terrible) and sell our father's insurance and mortgage business. Mary had worked for our father in the summer, and it fell to her to assume his office schedule, prepare the December premium notices and help the auditors who had come to assess Apollo Insurance and Mortgage's value. The auditors nearly abandoned the project. George McCutchan, who could afford a secretary only now and then, kept his own records in a nearly indecipherable hand. (The business eventually sold to a competitor in town, the father of one of my high school bandmates, who low-balled it and then forgot to send us our shares of quarterly commissions. We had to ask for them every time.)

I spent the days sifting through our parents' belongings—made runs to Goodwill, held a garage sale, placed a newspaper ad to find a home for Jonas. (His first adoptive family returned him because he snapped at a child. The second family presumably had an easier time.) I set items Mary and I would want to keep on a borrowed table in the middle of the living room, and each day when Mary came home from the office, we quietly decided who would take what. In the evenings we studied the reams of disorientingly itemized hospital bills that poured in, filled out opaque documents called insurance claims, wondered if the settlement from the Cadillac driver's company would cover outstanding debts and still send us back to college. (It did.)

The task I remember most clearly from those solemn nights was going through our parents' tan leather address book, a chaos of amendments after thirty years' use, and phoning their old friends in Maine and Washington to let them know what had happened. I considered writing letters instead, but something in me wanted to hear the voices of my mother's college roommate, my father's first business partner, the couple who lived next door to my parents when they first married. Many of these people I had met as a child, and I thought they might want to hear my voice, too. I think I was right about this, because after I introduced myself, whispered the news and absorbed the shocked response, each old friend wanted to know more about Mary and me: how old we were, where we went to school, what we were growing up to be. Some of them reminisced, offering gifts of anecdotes that unexpectedly pried open my parents' sealed pasts. From my mother's closest sorority sister I learned that Helen Bond had once been pinned to a football player who contracted tuberculosis, broke their engagement with a card and bouquet delivered by a florist, moved to Arizona to die, but eventually recovered, married somebody else, and returned to Maine to run his family's hardware store. I remember thinking how boring it would have been to be the daughter of a man who ran the same family business, decade after decade, and how proud I was to be the daughter of a man who took chances. This telephone conversation and all the others represented the closing of a circle, for beyond the following year's Christmas cards, with only one exception, Mary and I were never in touch with our parents' oldest friends again.

It was in the midst of this most delicate work that Eastern Airlines tracked us down on the telephone, and being our parents' daughters, Mary and I found Eastern Airlines' contrition over a dented casket ludicrous.

"Who cares if they MATCH?" I yelled, slamming down the telephone, my voice rebounding off the terrazzo floor. "They're going in the goddamned GROUND!"

Yeah!" Mary yelled, just as loudly. "Wouldn't Mom and Dad just HOWL at the idea!"

We collapsed on the sofa and laughed until our throats ached. Then we cried. Then we managed to laugh again. A few days later, an envelope arrived with Polaroid views of two caskets descending into a shady pocket of southern Indiana farmland. The attached note from an aunt read, "I am so sorry, girls, but the caskets did not match very well."

III

When Mary and I cleaned out the house, we decided I would keep our mother's family Bible, which originated with her father's mother. The family name is Marden, which is my mother's middle name, and mine, too. The cumbersome brown book, published in 1856, is falling apart; the eyes and forehead of an embossed gold Jesus have rubbed off. Inside, the family record of names, births, marriages and deaths is filled with exquisite penmanship, that is until you reach the entries I have made—I seem, in this department, to have inherited my father's disregard for appearances—each just-readable letter teeters with resistance to conventional posture. I have written in my birthdate and Mary's under the weathered inscription of Haverill's. That is the end of the page. There is no more space to write.

I do not know who will get this Bible after me. There is no parent to say who is deserving, no child to volunteer. Most relics I can take or leave, but a few command my devotion: grandmother Bond's good china, great-grandmother Bond's lamp table, the kitchen chair great-grandfather Hornby turned by hand. I have had every crack and nick in these things repaired, and although I am not a collector I am acquiring a collection. Mary has begun sending me her share of small heirlooms—our mother's brass cloverleaf paperweight, her cameo necklace—perhaps because she has not married and, as a freelance medical technician tends to move every couple of years. (Her last postcard came from Los Angeles: "Attending a professional meeting to see current computer software. Put on a Virtual Reality helmet and was linked up to a surgical procedure in Houston. Big F***ing deal!")

My cousins in Maine mail me shirtwaists our grandmother wore because, they say, the shirtwaists are my size.

If there is anything gained by losing your parents in your youth it is this: you are free to change your position in the family constellation because the old one no longer applies—unless, out of desire, fear, or inertia you imagine that it does. Mary is no longer the delicate one, and I am no longer the one of whom too much is expected. Yet I know the comfort, the illusion of sureness offered by a chrysaline role, and how long it can take to slough it off for something more authentic. After my parents' death I spent many years doing things I did not like simply because I was competent at them, acquiesced to relationships and ways of living that ate at my stomach, partly because I was used to being a person who is always depended upon, strong and predictable for others without questioning the price, a person compelled to maintain a reasonable, but always temporary, balance. A person so rooted in what appears to be an admirable moral stance finds true freedom terrifying.

When I finally began to claim that freedom I felt as if I were letting everyone down, most especially myself, whom I constantly confused with the person I had led others to think I was. I suspect that people whose parents are as fundamentally independent as mine were make the transition from outer to inner reliance earlier than I did. Perhaps losing my mother and father so suddenly at the exact time I was making that transition stalled me to some degree. I do not know that for certain. I only know that it seemed to take me a long time to ignore a good many distracting calls from without.

For a long time I did not want children. I had too

much to do on the clarinet, playing Beat The Clock, trying to perfect my apparatus before age and stress clarified limitations I suspected had always lain in the nerves of my wrists and back, the arch of my tongue. Techniques are the tools by which experience becomes singable, and while my weaknesses did not keep me from developing a professional career, they limited it. After awhile I could accept this because what mattered most to me was not a chair in the Cleveland Orchestra, but the ongoing discovery of new music, the more inventive, the better. In practice, as well as in concerts, I could lose myself in fresh, soaring melodies, surprising harmonic progressions, the delicate fluctuations in a single, held tone. I reveled in the polished, chameleonic possibilities of my instrument: the opaque, rubbery low register, the luminous, glistening highs. I craved the feeling of the fleshy centers of my fingertips dropping home smartly, stoppling holes smaller than dimes, smacking tear-shaped keys, scads per second. Although my fingers could fly as fast as most pieces required, I was partial to slow movements: noble, stretching lines, elegant disclosures of the spirit. In these, I would lean tenderly into each successive note of the lone voice, singing from a widening center. On the most blessed of days, I felt I was born to do this, that music, for me, was why, was why.

But as I approached my mid-thirties, I grew interested in creating a family. Part of it was my love for my second husband— warm, lively, imaginative, he would have been an excellent father. Yet I also fantasized, in the manner of a responsible first-born, about keeping the line going, sending forth splendid human beings named for Bonds or McCutchans, children my parents would have been proud of. I realized then that the death of your parents does not end your relationship with them, only changes it. Family expectations offer comfort, even when no one is around. My mother and father, gone for a decade, were powerful phantoms hovering about my shoulders, and I found myself shaking my fist at a new physical barrier.

The quest for children ended seven years later in a hospital conference room, when my husband and I, carrying the 1944 letter with Haverill's name in it, met with four other infertile couples and a nurse to discuss the upcoming "procedure." The two of us, laughing about something when we walked into the room, were shushed by the sight of eight miserable faces. Then the nurse said that for $6,000 a try, we had one chance in ten of conceiving a child in a Petri dish. I watched the sad couples brighten at these poor, expensively purchased odds, and recoiled. Outside the hospital, my husband, whose interest in children had subsided earlier when his composing career took fire, squeezed my hand and said, "We can still go on with it, if you want." I looked at him and answered, "This is where we stop. I want to do other things, instead."

Honoring limits in one area offers freedom in others, but release only comes when you hear a closing door press shut, feel the brisk snap of the latch. Not long after the hospital meeting, I went to the University of Texas Performing Arts Center to watch my husband conduct an orchestra concert for children. I barely made it—I'd lost track of time practicing a new, unaccompanied clarinet piece. I'd made these solos my specialty. They offered the most expressive freedom possible without having to rely on anyone else, and also the greatest risk. "Crater" on an unaccompanied solo, and you wither alone before hundreds of strangers; sing passionately come-what-may and you open, through the composer's creation, a rich, intimate world in which all can take part.

So, hurrying across wine-red carpeting to the interior

door of the UT concert hall, perspiring and breathless and emotionally raw, I was ill-prepared to be refused entrance by a fiftyish woman in a clown suit. "Sorry, ma'am," she said, perkily. "Adults are admitted only when accompanied by a child." Too stunned by the absurd injury to pull rank, I slipped into a little-used lounge and finally, deeply, wept.

My friend Nicky and I meet for lunch and I ask for the latest news of her lively mother, an 85 year-old widow with ample means, well-tended looks, and a fleet of boyfriends. Then I want to know about the children's activities: Jofka's furniture painting business, Gaby's riding lessons, Julian's Montessori class. I am interested in all of these things and yearn for similar reports to exchange with Nicky. I want to be able to say things like, "My mother wants to retire in Maine, but my father is set on Indiana," or "Dad said the other day that my face is beginning to look more like Mom's than his—what do you think?"

But alas, nearly twenty-five years have passed since my parents' accident, and my memories of them have not only dimmed, but changed with my own fickle tides. When I am at peace with the world, when it seems that typed sentences might express as much as the warm-blooded sweep of music can—maybe even, on good days, move bodies through space (appearances do help, after all)—I believe that I have long forgiven my parents for every misunderstanding and I swell with pride at their virtues. When I am out of sorts and temporarily lose the ration of self-possession my pen-sister Lydia became, my parents are responsible for whatever is wrong with me; they make convenient targets. Without flesh and blood to see, hear, smell or touch, it is easy to make somebody up, wrong. Indeed, it is the particular physical feature of a stranger—the silvery loft of hair on a poised, tall woman in a check-out line, the tanned, still-muscular arm of a tired, stocky businessman pushing seventy—that restores my parents most faithfully. In one gasp, I see again my mother or my father, Helen or George. The stranger feels my eyes, turns to look at me, and my heart pounds. What if it's them? Nonsense. The tall woman has brown eyes, not blue, the man's hairline doesn't start as far back as my father's did. I am relieved that the real world has snapped back, and disappointed that there are no miracles.

Right after it happened, I found the flimsiest excuses to work memories of them into conversation. I talked about them all the time, as if the force of my voice might enamel them permanently to the roof of my brain. My college friends at Michigan must have found me gruesome. Only one of them remains in touch. Don runs two transmission shops in Houston and has no interest in the fine arts—last spring he and his girlfriend went to Cancun and brought me a clay whistle shaped like a penis. I delight in his irreverence and admire his generosity—he recently adopted his troubled sister's teenaged son. A couple of times a year, Don and I meet for dinner in a chain restaurant off Houston's Katy Freeway, close to one of his transmission shops. We slide into a high-backed vinyl booth at Chili's or The Olive Garden, peruse sauce-spattered menus made large by boastful photographs of the entrees, and order the buffet. Then we load up our plates with soft bread, greasy salad and spaghetti bitter with oregano and reminisce about Ann Arbor, reeling off the names of beer joints we used to frequent: The Village Bell, The Pretzel Bell, a quiet corner of the Michigan Union's bar where I'd been able to unwind.

After awhile I fall silent and listen as Don talks at length of his failing parents, whom he loves, "typical Jews" he affectionately labels them, a retired toy manufacturer and his wife arguing their way into their eighties in a Brooklyn apartment. The latest tale is how Don tried to give them money to buy a television, which they refused because they said they hated TV. Unconvinced by their argument, Don paid a Brooklyn appliance dealer a large sum to deliver a fine color console to his parents' door. On the same day, they called him up to complain that the set wasn't big enough. "Some gift," they cried, "is it asking too much to have it fill completely that space next to the air-conditioner?"

What can kids make of their parents' sagas? What can they take from those vanishing lives?

Lately, I have been experimenting with a technique for wind instrument playing in which fresh air is drawn in through the nose at the same time that stored air in the lungs is released by mouth through the instrument. This technique, called circular breathing, allows the player to produce a continuous line of music like a violin does, without breaking the curve of a melody to inhale. It is possible, then, to play one piece of music, over and over, all in the same long, renewed breath.

Just so, like seasoned troubadours, Don and I croon continuously over the same old ground, imitating, ornamenting, sounding out rhymes. In this music there are so many details we want to hear, but at dinner, as new families breeze in to wait for clear tables, his folks tend to exit as crackling trumpets, while mine melt softly, like off-stage flutes. Over and over, we sing out for our parents, and over and over, we lose them.

FIVE SKETCHES WITH B

1976–2004

I

One sunny day when I was 26, I strode down the aisle of Tallahassee's First Methodist Church, escorted by Buxtehude's doughy setting of the St. Anne hymn, and listening to a voice in my head repeat a four-fold chant: "It will last, I want it to last, it might not last, it won't last." Brides before and after me have heard this voice; it often speaks from a sudden grasp of marriage's enormity, and falls silent as soon as the matching rings are exchanged, the fluffy white cake is cut.

But in my case, the voice spoke from well-founded doubt. My fiancé of two years had only recently challenged his elderly parents' objections to me, the first Yankee who would marry into their family, and I suspected his mother would continue to dominate him, even as we prepared to move to New Orleans, four states west of her antebellum perch in Georgia. Moreover, we were a balancing act: he a shy pianist and scholar fixated on research, I a new music performer and scattershot reader. As deeply as we cared for each other, his mother's influence, our youth, and our differences choked our growth as a couple, and over the next three years I felt increasingly marginalized and lonely. I didn't know it then, but I was ripe for an affair, and this is the tale of it and its curiously extended aftermath. The man who became my emotional lover, and something more than that, I will call B.

I met B at the first annual Texas-Louisiana Composers' Retreat, held at a farm in rural east Texas, close to the Louisiana border. The farmhouse and surrounding grounds, collectively called Morning Way, was the childhood home of a New Orleans arts patron who had offered his property for a week to eight university composers in the region. B, who taught at a school in Texas, was among them.

I came to the event as artist-in-residence—to collaborate with composers wishing to write for the clarinet, and at the end, to present a recital of contemporary music, with my husband at the piano. The chance to play for and mingle with so many creative musicians thrilled me, for during our three years in New Orleans, my husband and I had found scant interest in what one still referred to as the avant-garde. And while he was becoming less interested in playing, preferring instead the quiet life of scholarship, I was full of juice, organizing concerts in the Gothic-style churches along St. Charles Avenue, and flying off once a month for coaching in New York, where musician friends gave me tickets to the Met, the Philharmonic, and new music happenings. Each time I said good-bye to my husband and the plane lifted over the bayous, I imagined what it would be like to leave forever.

The year was 1979, the month January, the height of gray winter in east Texas, when the live oaks have surrendered all leaves to expose the gnarled twists of branches. All wildlife is mute, and the air is heavy with dampness. When my husband and I pulled in to Morning Way, the great farmhouse, to which several additions had obviously been made over the years, appeared exceedingly white and wet. A barn and a handful of utility buildings bordered the property, and across the gravel drive from the farmhouse crouched a green bungalow, where, I would learn later, the arts patron's nephew, a languorous fellow in his early thirties, lived by himself and tended a collection of Depression glass. The other composers would soon arrive; three of them I had heard of, and would later work with when I moved to Texas. But I had never heard of B, and there is no reason why anyone would know his name now, as much of his music remains unpublished, packed away in an archive at his school.

Inside the commodious house, decorated with floral wallpapers, oriental carpets and elaborately upholstered antiques, my husband and I were shown to an upstairs bedroom with a bath, and an adjoining parlor, where he would read and write. There were enough makeshift suites about the place for each composer to enjoy a similar arrangement. Meals at the retreat would run in the manner of an artist's colony: a sit-down breakfast of eggs, grits, pancakes and coffee in the kitchen at 7:30, pick-up sandwiches and iced tea available at noon, and dinner—usually fried chicken or pot roast with potatoes and green vegetables, and homemade cake or pie—at 6:30, in the dining room. All of this delicious Southern fare, flavored with plenty of syrup, lard, butter, and ham, was prepared and served by our patron's family cook, a local descendant of freed slaves. The only other woman at the retreat besides the cook and me was the wife of our school's music chair; she functioned in general as a hostess. I liked her, but secretly despised her traditional role, the sort my mother-in-law would have expected me to take. Yet I was grateful when she suggested everyone gather after dinner for drinks and talk in the library, where there were several comfortable couches.

My memory of the first evening is a blur of excitement, but I recall the second very clearly. I had spent the afternoon reading in the bedroom and come downstairs early to see if I might stake out more capacious headquarters in the library. It must have been around five o'clock, and I expected to have the room to myself. But there, sitting alone on one end of a green velvet sofa, was a dark-haired, bespectacled composer of about 40 who I'd met briefly the night before. B, rumpled and frowning, had balanced two books in his lap and was hunched over them intently, like a rabbi deciphering holy scripts. In his right hand, he held a large tumbler of liquor on ice.

What we spoke of I've long forgotten. Undoubtedly our conversation dwelled first on books and music, and moved on to the other occupants of the farmhouse. We both seemed to have noticed in detail the personal characteristics of our fellows and the lingering old-South atmosphere of Morning Way. He knew it before I did, that we were note-takers, observers, and performers who were also congenital loners. And so while I enjoyed his company, laughing more than I had in a long time, I didn't realize until the next day that somehow, I had become important to him, and that he would be important to me. I was sitting in a wing chair in the library, and in he strode, carrying what I would come to know as his ubiquitous glass of spirits. He stopped short in the center of the room and with those dark eyes stared at me—just stared—and with that stare drew me to him.

Were he alive, he might insist it was the other way around. We never will these things, we say. They are visited upon us: they just happen. But as the younger of the two of us, unaware of the depth of my unhappiness, still possessed of a Pollyanna-like enthusiasm for just about everything, and expecting nothing, I claim innocence.

    Matches made at artists' colonies are typically intense. So much structure slips away, and there you are, perhaps more "you" than you've been in a long while, or looked at another way, possibly less. If someone else, equally freed, recognizes a kindred spirit, a fire can kick up, fast. The "me" who recognized B was the questioning, adventuresome woman I'd been trying to stifle to make my marriage work. She was the real thing, and due for an outing. But with my husband always nearby or in the same room, nothing untoward was going to take place with B, who noted his sense of propriety. I, the peach ripe for plucking, tried very hard not to show that anything was going on with me. But how could I know if I succeeded? I was walking around in a thickening cloud of infatuation, sick and sweet.

    In the days that followed, B and I managed to bump into each other in the library, sit across from each other at dinner, and plop down next to each other when the group assembled in the evenings to play "Dictionary," which, with such an erudite crowd, was hilarious. I remember that B, drink in hand, fooled everyone with the word "cete," meaning "a company of beavers." During the days, B worked on a new piece for clarinet and piano. The first movement, titled "A Bundle of Wheat," he wrote start to finish in a single rainy morning. "I'll tell you what it means later," he said. We were standing outside under a dripping awning, where we'd collided, running from our cars to the house. Then he turned to me, wide-eyed, and in complete seriousness said, "We knew each other in a former life. Your name was Lydia."

    Had B offered any other name, I would have written him off as a drunk or a crazy. I did not believe in past lives then, nor do I now. But B's utterance shocked me into what would become a prolonged agitation, as Lydia was the name I had chosen for an alter ego when I was eleven years old. When I had a problem, I wrote a letter to Lydia, and then, as Lydia, I replied to myself with a big sister's advice. Lydia was the mysterious heroine of Kenneth Roberts' novel *Lydia Bailey*, which I had been reading at the time. Occasionally, I still wrote to her.

Speechless, I turned into the house, leaving B under the wet awning staring at me, and fled to the bedroom, where my husband was making lesson plans for a class he wouldn't begin teaching for two weeks.

"How can you waste such ideal practice time on Form and Analysis?" I cried.

"Is something wrong?" he replied, not looking up.

By the end of the week, B had completed a five-movement composition for clarinet and piano, about 20 minutes in length, titled *Five Sketches for Ann*. The attribution read, "By B, with Ann McCutchan," because, as he explained, my sound, my voice, and who he knew me to be had inspired him. "A Bundle of Wheat" was the only titled movement, but the whole work had a distinct narrative quality, the fifth movement weaving together restless, poignant themes from the previous four to create a sublime conclusion. On the last afternoon of the retreat, after my husband and I had given our program using the old Steinway in the formal living room, B and I premiered the *Sketches*, which we'd polished together in just two hours the day before. The other composers marveled at the quality of the work, the speed of its composition, and the symbiosis achieved by the two performers. "That piece is a keeper," everyone said.

II

All the way back to New Orleans, my husband kept his eye on the center line while I chattered, noting the homemade praline stands, the po-boy shacks, the sno-ball huts closed for the winter. When I ran out of road signs to read aloud, I tried to engage him in small talk, winning one-syllable responses. Finally, I gave up and studied the map.

Inside, my stomach rolled and churned with anticipation of what would happen next with B. The performance at Morning Way couldn't be the end of the story, although I had no intention of being unfaithful to the silent but honorable man sitting beside me. Two days after our return home, I received a letter from B, inviting me to his school six weeks hence to play a recital with him, including the *Sketches*. His wife, who I would later learn was planning to leave him, in part for his infidelities, was looking forward to meeting me, he said. "Fine with me if you go," said my husband, looking up briefly from his grade book.

So I accepted, and B responded immediately with a bulky envelope that barely made it through the mail slot. I told my husband it was just more music, pieces by other composers B thought we might play, but in fact, it was a 20-page letter and a packet of poems he had written, revealing the program behind the *Five Sketches*. It was a love story, of course, in another time, another place. The letter attested further to B's profound feelings for me, but also launched a compelling discussion of books and music. Had I read Pound? Did I know W.D. Snodgrass? Did I like Schoenberg's *A Survivor From Warsaw*? What were my favorite Schumann songs? His handwriting was a scrawl, loopy and exuberant. The depth of his ideas, his passion and insight, were beyond anything I had experienced, and, emboldened by his treatment of me as his intellectual equal, I replied with a mess of pages about HD and Dickinson, Webern and Brahms. Then, like an enthralled schoolgirl, I found his favorite authors and composers and devoured them. I bought a record album with Benita Valente singing B's favorite Brahms love song, *Meine Leibe ist grun*, and played it over and over, imagining it was being sung by B to me, as he intended. His phone calls came in the afternoons, when I was home alone, and the letters continued at such a rate that I rented a post office box to keep them secret.

In the middle of all of this, B sent me a copy of Fauré's song *Lydia*, reviving my uneasiness over that coincidence, and he composed another perfectly characteristic piece for me, a ruminating, scampish unaccompanied *Soliloquy*, the first sight of which caused me nearly to faint. For weeks I indulged in fantasies of Wagnerian scope, growing increasingly feverish, exhausted and panicky. Finally, I told myself, this had to stop. I was on the verge of becoming ill.

About a week before I was due to travel to B's school, I confessed everything to my husband, who was outraged—not at me, but at B.

"I knew something was going on," he shouted. "He's manipulating you!"

Grateful as I was for my husband's chivalry, I was still in thrall enough to want to protect B, and hated the idea that I was naïve, and that my husband, who I had viewed for some time as a social ostrich, knew it.

"No, he's not," I said. "It's just—"

"Just what?"

"It just got out of hand," I said, looking down at the floor.

But it was more than that; I was scared: scared that I cared for B more than I did my husband, and scared that B identified in his muse a far less conventional woman than the one my husband thought he was married to.

The next day I called B, who was full of news about activities surrounding our concert. He had reserved a motel room for me; there would be a reception in the concert hall and a party at his house. I told him everything sounded fine, but that we had to stop the letters.

"I can't do this any more," I murmured, afraid he would explode, like my husband had.

B was silent.

"It's not fair to my husband," I continued, gathering some strength. "I'm sending your letters back. Please destroy the ones I wrote to you."

"Are you sure?" he asked.

"No! Yes. I'm sure."

"I understand," he whispered. "All right."

I don't recall how I got from New Orleans to Texas. I must have driven west on I-10 to Lafayette and up through the swamps and villages of Cajun country to one of the crossings over the Sabine River. I rolled into B's town in and found his house with no trouble. He and his wife strolled out to greet me: she lovely and gracious, he with a tall drink in his hand, looking relieved to see me. She took my arm and said, with confidence, "I've heard so much about you. Come in and meet the children." Shuddering with the realization that B was at least as married as I was, and that his three teen-agers were real human beings the two of them had conceived and raised—an intimacy I knew nothing about—I let B's wife walk me into the house, where, beneath their modest chandelier, my fantasies quickly burned out, leaving the cold sweat of shame. As soon as we finished our pie and coffee, I explained that I needed to rest for the next day's rehearsal and concert.

"I'll lead you to your motel," B said.

What happened next was only the end of a possibility swirling quietly away. We arrived at the room and he held the door and followed me inside. He sat down on the double bed.

"I've been waiting for this," he said, sighing.

"I can't," I said, still standing.

He fell back, stared at the ceiling, and sighed deeply. "This is a once-in-a-lifetime chance," he said.

"I'm sorry. I can't," I repeated, growing a little frightened that he might force the situation.

But he didn't. He stared at me mournfully, sighed again, walked to the door, and spoke: "I'll see you tomorrow at rehearsal."

By the next morning, I had begun to recover my equilibrium. B and I would be colleagues, nothing more. At the concert, we threw ourselves into the music passionately, not as in a long-awaited union or a poignant farewell. It was better than that. For me, there was the sense that our artist-muse connection transcended what had been decided the night before—distance had restored the original, eloquent understanding. And I was relieved at having rescued myself from a predicament I couldn't have handled, and, in clear light, did not want. The next day I returned home to my husband, who dared not ask questions.

"Nothing happened," I volunteered. "And the concert was a success."

Now that we seemed to be out of danger, though, he grew recalcitrant and judgmental. I'd spent too much on a new dress, cooked the meat loaf too long, and when was I ever going to finish planting those camellias I'd chosen for the back yard? No matter how I approached him, loving or cool, direct or coy, he backed away, to my sorrow. His stance was a privilege he had earned for his suffering, and though I understood this, it was no less painful. When, brooding on what had happened, I suggested that we see a marriage counselor, he entrenched himself. "You may have a problem, but I don't," he said, snapping open his newspaper. "Go, if you like. I just hope it doesn't cost very much." Then he showed me a letter he'd written to his mother, announcing I'd had an "emotional affair" but was aware of my wrong turn and fully contrite. I was crushed—not that Mother knew (I could get over that) but that Mother still ruled my husband, and thus, our marriage. I could back out of an affair, but I felt helpless to fix this triangle.

A few months later, B composed one more piece for me: a trio for clarinet, cello and piano titled *Paramo Spring*; he wrote a poem to go with it about dry, barren landscapes. It was a terrible piece, and I never played it.

III

The story of B might have ended there, were it not for our geographical and professional proximity. A year and a half later, I saw him again. I had separated from my husband, moved to Texas, and begun work on a doctorate in a big prairie music school, where, with some fellow graduate students, I formed a new music ensemble. We wanted to make a tour of Texas and began calling possible hosts in the regions we hoped to visit. Since I no longer had to consider my husband, I contacted B, offering to repeat the *Five Sketches* with him on the program. He agreed, and reserved rooms for the group in the same motel, but now I had tour mates and he was newly married—giddily, it appeared—to a lab technician at his school.

I was feeling rather giddy myself, enjoying my independence, and the discovery of B's divorce and quick remarriage not only surprised me, it wised me up. It was possible, I realized, to share a certain depth of feeling and intellectual acuity with another person, without agreement on moral questions I thought important, nor similar temperaments. B was a depressive and an alcoholic, while I was an optimist whose claim to gastric excess was limited to a quarter-pound of chocolate once a month. I saw I had escaped not just a messy affair, but a second balancing act, for which B had auditioned another woman, one less ambitious, more maternal, than I. The new Mrs. B was a willowy beauty who spoke gently and favored simple, natural-fiber clothing. "He's told me lots and lots about you," she said. "I'm sure you know how much you mean to him." I nodded, suddenly perplexed. Did I mean that much to him, really? What had all of that been about, anyway?

The concert was a hit. At the house party afterward, B spoke to me at length, his sentences a river of slurs, until my ensemble's percussionist, who many years later would confess to having been jealous, brought me a plate of crackers and Mrs. B's excellent, garlicky hummus. A few months later B came to my school for a professional meeting and stopped by my apartment for a glass of wine. We sat cross-legged on the dank shag carpeting, because I had no living room furniture, only two thousand record albums stacked against the walls. I jabbered about my studies and career plans, and he gave me a wan, indulgent smile. Then he said he couldn't believe it had been two years since the composer's retreat, "since all of those amazing things happened," as he put it. I smiled indulgently, too, for I thought I had put the event well enough behind me, and if by chance he was angling for my sympathy and another opportunity . . . but why would he do that now? For the moment, I decided he was overly sentimental or clinically depressed. I offered him a second glass of wine. He drank it, hugged me, and left. A few more months passed, and he called again. He had been invited to perform one of his pieces on a university concert in Austin—would I meet him there and do the *Five Sketches* again?

By now I had a clearer sense of B's work and how it fit into his life. He composed constantly for whoever was at hand (his new wife, an amateur singer, inspired a collection of songs, including settings of some Millay poems I had sent him) but he published very little. I am not sure why, for his music was tonal and attractive, and might have caught some attention. Several times I heard him deride the music publishing industry. Either he had tried to publish and failed, or was simply given to dashing off one piece, fulfilling the score in performance, and moving on to the next project.

I also came to know more of his history. B was born in Arkansas and raised southern Baptist, which might explain his aversion to organized religion. He could be nastier than anyone I knew on the subject. He and his first wife married right out of high school when she became pregnant. The other children followed quickly, as B worked and went to college; he finished a doctorate and took the job in Texas. B hand-built most of the rambling redwood contemporary house he and his family lived in, and was legendary among students and faculty for pissing off of the deck. He was the kind of musician who always has an auxiliary obsession that changes every few years. B's were racing bikes, computers, cultivating antique roses, and finally, assembling a German dictionary from scratch. Friends and colleagues found him both lovable and irritating. His sharp wit and droopy-eyed cynicism were well known, as were his bad moods and untempered disgust with academia's plodding bureaucracy. Still, he knew how to work the system, and in the last years of his tenure, he enjoyed an endowed professorship for which "he didn't really have to do anything," as one of his fellow teachers put it. He was happy surrounded with books, music, and the materials for a project, but he also couldn't stand to live alone. When he was between wives he monopolized his friends' time at all hours, at least once going so far as to leave his house at 3 AM, roam the neighborhood, and knock on a colleague's bedroom window, demanding he join him for a beer.

In Austin, B and I ran through the *Sketches* just twice

before taking the stage. The performance went exceedingly well—as well as the farmhouse premiere two years before—and I was surprised to have submerged myself so completely. This time, though, we were simply two compatible performers whose interpretations of the piece meshed perfectly, recreating music that had been composed by others, in another time and place. Afterward, the organizer of the concert, a tall, lean composer, sidled up to me and asked pointedly if I was having an affair with B. When I denied it, he said, "The way you play together? I don't believe you!" and winked.

The party afterward was held at a sprawling hilltop home west of the city, with an outstanding nighttime view. The host, yet another university composer, made a show of bringing out a cookie sheet of dried, homegrown marijuana, and those interested in rolling a joint had to separate the seeds and stems. The walls vibrated with pounding music, escalating talk, and the occasional stomp or scream meant to emphasize a point and grab attention from those attempting more subdued exchanges. The assortment of guests included everything from a heavily-endowed flute player who posed jauntily before the cheese tray in a pink t-shirt with BITCH stenciled across the front, to a professor emeritus who trembled in a corner, adjusting his hearing aid. I stood at the entrance to the scene with B and his wife, and all three of us agreed we'd prefer to find a bar for a quiet drink — but not before the tall composer, unbuttoning his shirt, flitted up briefly to flirt with me and announce he was about to dive naked into the host's swimming pool.

"He's kind of cute," I said, taking in the tall composer's wavy yellow hair. The successful performance had lit up my audacious streak. I was single now, wasn't I?

"Yes, he is cute," Mrs. B agreed.

"I don't like him," B muttered, turning toward the door.

A few months later, I learned that the tall composer had separated from his wife, and then, at a summer festival out west, I took up with him. Not long afterward, on my way to an audition, I passed through B's town and stayed the night. In the morning I felt ill and Mrs. B accompanied me to the local hospital, where the doctor, surely a Bible-thumper, eyed my Indian print skirt and Ralph Waldo Emerson t-shirt, questioned my recent activities, and misdiagnosed a minor stomach ailment as an STD. B stayed out of the discussion that followed, only growled as I left the house, "Just don't marry that guy."

But I did.

IV

Seven years passed. I had made a life in Austin, playing with various musical groups and writing for the newspaper. My energetic union with the tall composer had run aground early on—if before I had paired up with Ashley from *Gone With The Wind*, this time I had chosen Updike's *Rabbit*. But I loved the tall man and was determined to hang in, telling myself that as long as I focused on my work, and the travels and musical projects we shared, it would not be true that I had become another accommodating faculty wife, applauding her husband's promotions and looking the other way.

One day in August, B called and invited me to apply for a job at his school teaching clarinet. The long-time instructor there had been dismissed suddenly from his studio and assigned music appreciation classes, the usual fate of someone who just can't cut it any more. I hadn't taught in a while, missed it, and was glad for the opportunity when it was offered. I would cover my lessons in two packed days, driving over one morning and returning the next evening.

I remember with pleasure the early morning drives, which commenced well before sunrise, progressing east out of Austin, through the little farm towns of Thorndale and Rockdale, and over the Brazos River to Hearne, where cotton bales the size and shape of freight cars lay in fields of glistening stubble. The big orange Texas sun had ascended by then, and the town's diners were surrounded with pickups; after I'd stopped at the one before the railroad station for coffee, I nearly always had to wait, arms resting on the steering wheel, for the Union Pacific to pass. Sometimes I took an indirect route, through Franklin, where on Main Street there was a Carnegie Library, and a low, uneven attachment to it labeled Carnegie Hall, where I always intended to have my picture taken, but never did. Once I bought the local paper there and read that a wedding had been attended by, among others, one Louisa T. Moultree, and her dog, Brandy, both residents of Dime Box.

  B and his wife had invited me to stay each week in one of their extra bedrooms, as B's children were now off at college, or working. I never saw much of B, though. The school had recently given him an electronic studio in a building a block away from Music, and that is where he hid out, making new pieces that seemed to be several steps behind what the rest of the world was doing, and beginning the German dictionary, inspired by one of his daughter's trips to Munich.

  Mostly, I got to know better Mrs. B, who had grown tired of lab work and was starting a technical writing business. She also devoted a lot of time to a particular Buddhist nun, for whom she had turned one of the spare bedrooms into a meditation shrine. I grew very fond of her, enjoying our early breakfasts, surrounded by the many houseplants she cared for in the sunny, glassed-in living room B had fashioned years ago. In agreeable silence we would pull apart the fresh, healthy muffins she had baked to go with our coffee, and converse about macrobiotics, spiritual quests, and her young son and daughter, who also lived there and were beginning to show musical talent. We spoke of breast cancer, too, as she feared it; it ran rampant in her family.

  At the end of the school day, I would go out to dinner, alone or with a colleague, so as not to burden Mrs. B with entertaining me. Later at the house, I might find B in the living room, drinking and reading. Most times I greeted him softly and slipped back to my room. His cynicism, formerly leavened with humor, now seemed absolute, and he appeared always to be idling, summoning no more than the energy required to shuffle across the room and freshen his glass.

At the same time, though, I was, fully ten years after the composers' retreat, still aware of a kind of bond between us. Mrs. B sensed it and rightly trusted its dormancy, my high interest in other pursuits, and my warm friendship with her. My husband sensed it, and knew he could count on me to take the high road. He had never been confident of his own appeal, though, neither had he proven to be at ease with a talented wife, and, like B, couldn't stand to be alone. By then he had begun a series of liaisons with worshipful students; that year he brought one home on nights I was away.

By the end of the spring term my husband had negotiated a two-year position in Honolulu, and I, too exhausted by our marriage to step out of it, resigned from my teaching job to accompany him. Maybe, I desperately theorized, living in paradise would transform us; Pélé would put a torch to the past and we would return to Texas, a solid couple. (I would be wrong.)

In those years, and the ones that followed, I rarely thought of B, until a friend at his school happened to relay some news. One summer in the mid-1990s, while B was away visiting relatives, Mrs. B underwent, without his knowledge, a prophylactic mastectomy and left B for an old friend who had attended her in the hospital. After a few months of miserable boozing, B met and hastily married a newly hired sociology professor, also in her 50s, who shared his taste for drink.

I met B's last wife soon after their wedding. Once again, I was passing through town, this time on the way to a magazine assignment in Mississippi, and we three met for lunch in one of those heavily treed mansions-turned-restaurants the Old South is deservedly famous for. The third Mrs. B had a pleasingly dry sense of humor, but lacked the grace and charm of her predecessors, speaking distractedly about her research in a smoke-husky voice. I tried my best to follow, occasionally stealing a glance at B, who had sunk into a red-wine reverie. After lunch, he invited me to his studio to pick up some books about composing. I had just begun writing one on composers and creativity. It would focus on successful Americans in the prime of their careers; the question of including B never came up. In the studio, B gathered a huge stack of volumes, some of them more than thirty years old, packed them in boxes, and carried them out to the trunk of my car. He had given me his entire composition library. It was all over for him.

  Two years later, I was managing funds for a service organization and had to choose a representative from B's region for a grants panel. Mrs. B expressed interest and held the credentials, so I invited her. She and B drove to Austin for the weekend of evaluations, but I never saw him, not even at the opening reception, to which spouses were invited. In the first round of rankings, Mrs. B doggedly challenged the majority's opinion with meaningless criticism, and skewed the voting, making adjustments necessary later. At lunchtime, I caught sight of the flask tucked into the side pocket of her briefcase.

V

For a long time now, I had conflated my original affection for B with disappointment in his weaknesses and a selfish curiosity about how his life would play out. I couldn't help comparing our physical positioning in the world; while he had remained in the same spot for decades, I had proven to be a traveler. I'd sensed this difference from the beginning—it spoke of much more than bodily location, of course—and was one of the reasons I could never envision actually living with him. In much less time than it took his first and second wives, I would have bolted.

I spoke to B once more, in the summer of 1999. I had finally left my husband and was on my way to New York for a year, to teach writing. I couldn't bear to stop by the house, so I called B from the road. I started to explain why my marriage was over, and he cut me short. "I told you so," he said. Something very old passed between us then. There was nothing more to say.

The composer book was published that fall and I sent B a copy; he replied with an email, inviting me to visit him and Mrs. B in Germany, where they had begun to spend the summers. His note sounded surprisingly upbeat, so I was tempted—might there be another chapter, one in which he would find clear-eyed contentment, and I would warmly express the best of my old sentiment for him? For, as I had come to understand, he had long ago served as *my* muse, acknowledging me as a creative and intellectual colleague, giving me the initial confidence to go beyond interpreting the work of others, to create work of my own. But I wasn't settled financially and couldn't afford a trip overseas.

Four years later, after I'd moved again, to teach in Wyoming, the composer book was issued in paperback, and I sent a mass email to announce it. A reply came immediately from Mrs. B: "Call me." I did. B had died the previous spring of a massive heart attack. He had gone to the bathroom in the middle of the night; the next morning she woke to the sound of water rushing from a faucet and discovered him on the floor. "I tried to contact you then," she said, her voice aslosh with confusion. "We all knew you were special to him. But the last address I had for you was in Ithaca." Weeping softly—for her, for B, for my own lost husbands and the lurching passage of time—I accepted this, though I knew well she could have found me through friends or the Internet. Then she asked if we could exchange some writing. "Of course," I said, wanting to extend my hand. I sent her an article, but she never responded in kind, neither did she tell me she had lost her job, and was living alone in the house with the glass living room.

A former colleague and close friend of B's described the memorial service for me: "There were all kinds of people getting up and telling the same old stories, like about B pissing off the deck," he said. "This went on for an hour and a half. When it finally got to be my turn, I decided not to say anything so they could get the damn deal over with. Afterward I told his children that if B had been there, he would have left an hour ago."

Last January marked 25 years since the first annual Texas-Louisiana Composer's Retreat, which was discontinued in 1982. One day in March, I was searching for my name on the Internet, as authors often do, looking for new reviews. Up came a reference to an archive at B's school, and this entry: "*Five Sketches for Ann*, by B, with Ann McCutchan. Original ink manuscript." I froze in my chair. They couldn't have it, because I do. B gave it to me; it is the score I performed from; even he had played from a Xerox. But what bothered me even more was the possibility that a second ink copy I hadn't known about might reveal to anyone B's program, including the playful, romantic notes he had written to indicate what each musical gesture, especially those in the final movement, meant. Some details of love stories must stay with those who lived them. How relieved I was to receive the archivist's answer to my query: "There are no writings of any kind on this score."

❧ THREE BAGATELLES ❧

American Beethoven / 1985

In the mid-eighties I worked for a year as a freelance arts journalist in Rochester, New York, home of the Eastman School of Music, and early on, a history geek in the hallowed halls told me a relative of Ludwig van Beethoven (1770–1827) was buried in one of the city cemeteries. In less time than it takes to belt the opening motive of the Fifth Symphony, I was chasing that story headfirst down a crooked path of research, finally gaining no more than a fifty-page notebook of bewildering "facts" and five extra pounds around the waist from spending too much time in libraries.

Briefly, I considered suing the geek for damages.

Yet I had to admit the chase had been fun. Who doesn't love a mystery, anyhow? True, the day spent combing the Monroe County cemetery records was a bust. But the moment "Beethoven, Ludwig" surfaced in the 1872 Rochester City Directory was a blast.

Had TV been invented in the 19th century, the Beethoven family would surely have starred in a soap opera. Though the composer of the Eroica symphony never married, his line extended through his troubled nephew Karl, for whose guardianship Beethoven wrangled *fortissimo* with Karl's mother Johanna, the wife of Ludwig's deceased brother, Casper.

Ludwig, who judged others as quickly as he quaffed bottles of wine, felt that Johanna was morally unfit for motherhood; he often referred to her as "The Queen of the Night." Some analysts of the four-year spat see Beethoven's preoccupation with his nephew as a substitute for romantic commitment, but then, those experts may be the kind who believes every passion not directly related to marriage is a substitute for it. Anyway, Ludwig had evidence that Johanna lacked proper mothering skills, and resolved to triumph.

Beethoven eventually won the legal battle, but by then, poor Karl was so confused by the debacle that he'd begun hanging around a pack of characters his uncle did not approve of. Apparently Karl's friends helped drive him farther to the edge. In 1826, at the age of 18, he attempted suicide with a shot to the head, and failed. Uncle Ludwig died a year later from unknown causes. (In 2005, advanced X-Ray technology revealed lead poisoning as the culprit.) As if orchestrating a happy ending, Karl moved on to become a reputable gentleman, marry, and father five children.

Yet Karl's only son, who carried the name of the famous composer, carried as well the family's seeds of scandal—all the way to Rochester.

According to the handful of scholars who have investigated the matter, the second Ludwig van Beethoven, born 1839 (and hereinafter referred to as American Beethoven to differentiate him from the famous composer), was a bright, cunning man who used his pedigree to gain generous financial support from the king of Bavaria. He also traded on his name in another way: by selling fake relics and souvenirs of his granduncle. One wonders what sorts of items he peddled—500 quill pens all supposedly used to compose the opera *Fidelio?* Beer steins inscribed, "I Love the Moonlight Sonata"? Unfortunately, nobody knows for sure.

The law got wind of American Beethoven's fiddling, but by that time he, his wife Marie, and their small son, another Karl, had fled to America. They arrived in New York City on September 15, 1871, and proceeded to Rochester that same night. Musicologist Paul Nettl wrote in 1957 that American Beethoven's second son, Heinrich, was born a week after the family's arrival in the United States, died six months later and "was buried in the cemetery at Rochester."

That's the grave I couldn't find. I couldn't even figure out which cemetery it was in.

The 1871 Rochester City Directory says American Beethoven and Marie lived at 21 Prospect Street on a block now consumed by a low-income housing project—just around the corner from Melody Street. It gives American Beethoven's occupation as "teacher," but I couldn't find his name on any faculty roster published by public or private schools of the time. It's possible he was employed by the *Real-Schule* for German-speaking students, of which no faculty list seems to exist. Marie is described in the directory as "music teacher, Livingston Park Seminary," but nowhere in the Rochester Public Library's archives of that now-defunct academy for young ladies could I discover records of her position. Perhaps no one connected with the seminary wanted to document it, because sometime during the single year the Beethovens lived in Rochester, they were both sentenced to prison in Vienna *in absentia*. Nettl believed that the nearly 8000 German-born Rochesterians (one-eighth of the city's population) read of the scandal in *Nachrichten,* the

German-language newspaper published in New York City.

So the Beethovens picked up and moved to Buffalo for a brief time. Later reports trace them all over the Upper Midwest, from Hamilton, Ontario, to Sabula, Iowa. For a while, Marie was a popular concert pianist in Canada. But the legendary name ran hot through North America, and in 1874 American Beethoven shuttled his family to Manhattan and changed the last name to von Hoven. "Louis von Hoven" became the highly successful managing director of a European-style messenger service, impressing the public with such respectable accomplishments as providing 500 wheelchairs for the elderly at a state fair.

There's a pattern here with the Beethoven men: bad boy behavior and a turn for the better. One wonders what upbeat music the original Ludwig would have composed had he not departed this world so soon after writing the "Ode to Joy."

What ultimately happened to American Beethoven is unclear. Sometime before 1890, he mysteriously moved his family to Paris and probably died there. In the end, Rochester turned out to be merely a way-station for a bunch of Beethovens running from the law. That probably explains why there is no record of baby Heinrich, who may have been interred anonymously to avoid calling attention to the family.

But I'll always wonder why these musical fugitives first picked Rochester as their hiding place. The population of the city in 1870 was only 62,424—perfect for proliferating gossip. And although the large German-speaking community surely beckoned, the Beethovens must have known their countrymen would out them. It wouldn't have taken long for their neighbors to start asking each other, "Who is that guy named Beethoven? You know, the one who says he owns the original score of the Emperor concerto?"

Bayou Postcard / 1999

Driving to New Orleans a few weeks ago, I grew weary of I-10 and swung down onto US 90 at Lafayette for a change of scenery. Arcing over the Atchafalaya River bridge east into Morgan City, I decided to bend my route once more and headed north on LA Route 70, following signs to Brownell Memorial Park, a wildlife sanctuary on the banks of Lake Palourde.

Brownell Memorial Park, I discovered, is a 9.5-acre bayou refuge perfect for back-road idlers like me who prefer the surprises of indirect paths with no road signs and lots of greenery. The park is filled with thick patches of ferns, explosions of wildflowers, and graceful stands of moss-draped cypress that cast winged shadows onto Palourde's dark, undulating surface. Egrets, blue herons and pelicans swoop in and out, and silent alligators ply the waters, their ridged eyes just visible above the gumbo. But what truly took my breath away in this quiet retreat was the inexplicable presence of a carillon tower, a 106-foot concrete column topped by a nest of bronze bells, rising up out of the swamp like a prophecy.

The carillon, commissioned in the early 1970s by Claire Horatio Brownell, the park's benefactor, is one of the world's largest. Its 61 bells, ranging in weight from 18 to 4730 pounds, were cast in Holland by Petit & Fritsen, the oldest bell foundry in Europe. When I asked park supervisor Earl Robicheaux about the carillon, he told me the magnificent bells have barely been played since the tower's construction, and ring the hours only by way of an electronic impulse. It seems that the Brownell

Foundation, which operates the park, has had problems funding carillon performances, and until recently has been unable to serve the carillon's natural destiny. When I lamented the waste of a world-class instrument, Robicheaux offered me a tour, and so inside and up we went, climbing spiraled steps to the tower's crown, where the clavier, or "keyboard" of the carillon sits, its two ranks of wooden batons roughly corresponding to the keys on a piano. To see the bells, I had to wiggle up through a trap door in the clavier room's ceiling to open air, and it was well worth the vertigo to admire the bells and enjoy a breezy, commanding view of Lake Palourde.

I was drinking in the soft, magnolia-scented air when, without warning, the huge bells beside and above me began to clang and chong. They weren't chiming the hour or intoning a hymn, but punching out vibrant clusters of harmony, sonic pillars for a hypnotic, unmistakably French melody that slowly unraveled and floated out over the cypresses. Curious to observe the source, I dropped down through the trap door just in time to see the park supervisor hammer a last handful of clavier batons.

"What was that beautiful piece?" I asked.

"I wrote it," Robicheaux admitted. "It's called *Music for Egrets.*"

So here was another surprising presence in Brownell Memorial Park. Earl Robicheaux, it turned out, is a composer. He grew up in Berwick, one town away from the Port of Morgan City, then left Louisiana for twenty years to live and work in other places. Along the way he earned a doctorate in music, and about a year ago he came home to Cajun heartland to care for his elderly mother and work as Brownell Memorial Park's supervisor and first music director. Robicheaux's biggest task now is building financial support for renovating the moth-balled carillon so the park can offer public concerts. He envisions a series that includes visiting soloists, complementary instruments (such as a brass choir), and new, experimental pieces. The carillon, he feels, has the potential to become cultural manna, as enriching to the soul as crawfish to the belly or oil to the pocketbook.

"The carillon's importance lies in providing for an environment where man and nature interrelate," Robicheaux explained carefully, as if reading from a finished speech. As it turns out, he is an environmental advocate, too. "The carillon sound itself is non-obtrusive to its surroundings," he continued. "I think of it as a gentle sonic beacon—a lighthouse of sound, if you will. Its resonances blend with the sounds of birds, frog choruses, the wind and water. I think it shows how man and nature can coexist in subtle harmony, as opposed to man's alienation from nature, which seems so common now."

We sat in silence, listening to the wind gust around the bells overhead. Then we descended the tower. Robicheaux went on to greet a young man and woman planning their wedding in the park, and I walked some distance down a caliche trail to admire the ferns. A few moments later, I turned to regard the carillon once more. The late afternoon sun had transformed the concrete tower into a gold obelisk, overlaid with the dark hand-prints of a mimosa's shadow. I hoped that the carillon, a descendant of Old World chimes, would sing and sing again. In the hands of a good composer who loves the land he attends, the Brownell carillon could one day seem as indigenous to Louisiana as a name like Robicheaux, *Danse de Mardi Gras*, and the bayou itself.

Welcome to the Kingdom / January 7, 1995

Tomorrow is the 60th anniversary of Elvis Presley's birth, a time to reflect on the significance of His existence, and how it has touched each and every one of us, deeply and meaningfully, in all of its incarnations.

For each of us treasures a Most Meaningful Elvis. I prefer to fixate on Beach Idol Elvis as he appeared in Blue Hawaii, et al, open-shirted and greasy with all that Wildroot, before Liberace urged him to suit up like an extra for *Plan Nine From Outer Space*. (True fact. Check out the Elvis correspondence at the Liberace Museum in Las Vegas.) There's also G.I. Elvis, Kid Galahad Elvis, and, praise the Lord, Gospel Elvis.

No matter which Elvis one worships, one can't honor him enough on this occasion. So last week, in tribute to the Hunk of my burning puberty and His untimely forfeit of membership in the AARP, I toured Graceland Too, an offbeat shrine in Holly Springs, Mississippi, in the netherland between Tupelo, his birthplace, and Memphis, where Elvis died at the age of 42. Graceland Too, it turned out, holds every manifestation of The King ever imagined.

The home copier quality brochure I picked up at the Holly Springs Chamber of Commerce described Graceland Too as an "1853 auntebellum (sic) home." Yet the white-columned mini-mansion's charm unquestionably rests with the unrelenting quantity of Elvis memorabilia displayed—the 40-year collection of proprietor Paul MacLeod, then 53.

"I have been an Elvis fan since I was thirteen years old," MacLeod told me. "The first time I ever seen Elvis was on the

CBS Stage Show with the Dorsey Brothers. I have known from that moment I would always be a big fan."

MacLeod isn't an ordinary devotee. All five ground floor rooms of the manse at 200 East Gholson are jammed so tight with Elvis stuff it would take an exorcist to clean house. Posters, lamps, buttons, trading cards, concert tickets, jewelry, you name it, Elvis sulks from it.

MacLeod has striven to capture the spirit of the original Graceland with decorative touches such as gold, ball-fringed swag drapes and a white-and-gold ceramic cherub bearing an Elvis pillow. Admittedly, his collection has driven out any real furniture. In one room, a mannequin sporting a Sun Records t-shirt oversees hundreds of discs and record jackets shingling the walls. Across a passageway, an ill-lit throng of urns, dried floral arrangements and giant satin hearts prove MacLeod was once among the privileged invited to choose from the $35,000 worth of tributes heaped at Elvis' grave.

Even the ceilings droop with newspaper articles, Elvis stamps and commemorative bubblegum wrappers.

Despite this colorful abundance, MacLeod focuses his collection on print and broadcast material and claims to have the largest independent Elvis archive, including 22,000 newspaper clippings, 10,000 film clips, and a few treasured feet of microfilm. Much of this library is stacked about the house in color-code binders, boxes, and trunks. MacLeod, along with his son, Elvis Aaron Presley MacLeod, converted the kitchen into a recording studio, where the pair monitors radio stations day and night for references to The King. The pantry is crammed with mail and notebooks. "We go out to eat," Elvis, 21, explained.

The former dining room hosts a wall of television sets and VCRs, where the father-son team channel-surfs for Elvis sightings around the clock. Since 1981 the MacLeods have burned out nine TVs, nine VCRs, and one Mrs. MacLeod, who three years ago declared, "It's either me, or Elvis." The MacLeods say they don't know where she went.

Young Elvis, who said his last credit card application was turned down because the bank deemed it a hoax, enjoys reciting facts for the visiting faithful. Elvis' original hair was blond; he died it black in 1957 so he'd look like Tony Curtis. Elvis once was hospitalized for fingernail gouges after fans rushed the stage in Windsor, Ontario. A bottle of Elvis wine corked one month after his death now sells for $2500. Of the 30,000 Elvis impersonators worldwide, a man who attended Ole Miss ranks No 7. Elvis Too takes additional pride in proffering the day's mail: letters from collectors all over the globe, as well as bits of publicity for Graceland, Too.

"Here's a newsletter from a polyurethane company," he said, brandishing a black-and-white pamphlet. "We're in it. They make lamination, plastic bags? And there we are."

During my visit, the MacLeods told me they were composing a database of their resources and intended to go online with it, though Elvis admitted they're "paranoid about viruses."

Meanwhile, the world keeps coming to them, via satellite, filler-seeking film crews from Geraldo and Good Morning America, and folks curious enough to follow U.S. 78 or Mississippi Route 7 into Holly Springs.

Graceland, Too is open to the public at $5 a head, but I learned from an insider whose mother was good friends with Eudora Welty that it's best to ring up for an appointment.

The MacLeods, both attired in black the day I stopped by, prefer to dress for visitors in replicas of Elvis outfits sewn up for them by local seamstresses. They also give generously of their time and talent. At the close of my 90-minute tour, Paul MacLeod treated me to his own rendition of *Hound Dog*, hips and all. After which I strolled into Holly Springs' town square, ordered a cheeseburger in one of two cafes, and got the waitress to put her cigarette down long enough to tell me what she thinks of Graceland, Too. But that's another story.

AFTERMATH

1996

> *There is no reason to believe that everything in a life—each thought, feeling, action, dream—can be linked, or must fit in. It is the making coherent of a life—the forcing of a pattern—that people often suffer from.*
> —Adam Phillips, *Terrors and Experts*

A thunderstorm shook Bastrop County early Friday morning, a sky-cracker that knocked out power to the northwest and sent pinecones hurtling to our back deck like hand grenades. In the tops of trees, lightning fluttered—Zeus playing with the light switch. I couldn't sleep, and neither could my two big dogs. Kiri huddled in a corner, Jake flattened himself under the bed, and I cowered in the sheets, dandling a remote control, tracking the storm on television, the way my husband, a traveling composer, might. For two hours, KVUE's Doppler Radar painted the storm red, an enraged paramecium lurching southeast toward Houston.

Hours later, I strolled outside. The deck, 'though caked with bark and pine needles and green cones, was unharmed, and at the front of the house, my flowers and herbs stood tall in the sun, with the exception of a top-heavy young fig, which bowed low as if a king had passed. No big deal, that storm. A run of ruckus, a heap of hoo-hah.

But rounding the corner to the garage, I discovered a monstrous oak, the huge, moss-bearded veteran that had dictated the curve in the driveway, lying on its side, filling the concrete pad with greenery. All fifty feet of the old man, all length and width and depth, had toppled in the wind onto the drive and across into the weak arms of young pines.

Another homeowner might have clenched her jaw and begun figuring the cost of the old man's removal, but I confess I was elated. LOOK, will you LOOK! I shouted out loud to no one. My delight at the surprise was so complete I felt, for a moment, as if my cells might leap into a wild habañera.

Throughout the morning (while a stout man in slippery jeans dismembered the tree with a chainsaw) I found myself replaying the first sight of the fallen timber over and over, wishing to gasp again with surprise and pleasure, like a young girl re-living her first kiss. I wanted to isolate that shock, I wanted to pinch it between my thumb and forefinger, hold it up like a rare bud or a firefly to prolong the glow. But I couldn't, of course. The tongue you don't expect darts into your mouth just once.

Still, the memory of the downed oak continued to startle me, and in the days since the storm I have committed outlandish and unpremeditated deeds: worn a fancy white blouse to dine in an Italian restaurant, purchased an expensive hand-tinted photograph at an art show, prepared fried eggs, hot sausage and white-flour biscuits for breakfast. Yesterday I removed the clumsy, ill-prescribed orthotics from all of my shoes, instructed a hysterical colleague of mine to button her lip and waited until midnight to do the grocery shopping. This morning in my study I pulled out all of my carefully categorized books, piled them in the middle of the floor, and dawdled among them all day, finally sticking them back onto the shelves in no particular order. Now reference and fiction and philosophy and the lives of musicians stand shoulder to shoulder, and not alphabetized. Frank Zappa towers over Aristotle, Faulkner tolerates *Arabic At A Glance*.

In an interview about his composition *Child of Tree*, in which musical sounds are produced on cacti, John Cage said, "I'm finding ways to free the act of improvisation from taste and memory and likes and dislikes. If I can do that, then I will be very pleased. In the case of plant materials, you don't know them; you're discovering them. So the instrument is unfamiliar. If you become very familiar with a piece of cactus, it very shortly disintegrates, and you have to replace it with another one you don't know. So the whole thing remains fascinating, and free of your memory as a matter of course."

One of Cage's most famous works, *4:33*, calls for a pianist who strides on stage, positions himself at the bench, sits silently for exactly four minutes and thirty-three seconds, then walks off. Those who have never witnessed a performance of this piece find the exercise shocking. Reactions range from embarrassed titters (What's going on?) to harumphs of indignation (I paid good money for this seat!). But always, by minute two, the nervous responses dissipate. People begin to listen to what else there is to hear: the rustle of concert programs, the howl of a heating system, the sizzle of hosiery.

I met Cage the year before he died, at an 80th birthday concert in San Francisco. The concert was held in a lovely old downtown cathedral, and there was a reception afterward in the church basement. Several music students had put out plates of American cheese and Triscuits, alongside a punchbowl of lemonade. I, who had seen lesser composers honored with king crab and ice sculptures, wondered snidely why someone hadn't done a better job. Cage approached the refreshment table with obvious delight. "This looks delicious," he said.

Lately I have been wondering how I can guarantee myself enough surprises to last another forty-five years. The mid-life dalliance I swore was not textbook has already occurred, and when I hear of others' escapades I grow weary recalling the difficulty of concealment, the radioactive soup of grief.

A friend says I am lucky—two reckless weekends drove his first wife to another state, and now, having begun a second family, he's afraid even to look a pretty bank teller in the eye.

Then again, one married pair I know unravels quite regularly. Last year, Mr. Fitch placed a provocative ad with *The Classical Music Lovers Exchange* and commenced a titillating affair of words with a lady 1500 miles away. When Mrs. Fitch found out, she hired a marriage counselor and they worked out a deal: Mrs. Fitch guaranteed Mr. Fitch twice-weekly sex in exchange for a retraction of his, er, ad. This year, Mrs. Fitch took up with another woman, who forced her to choose between herself and Mr. Fitch. Mr. Fitch found out and confronted the lesbian lover. Mrs. Fitch fell apart. Realizing he had the upper hand, yet feeling the need to strengthen it, Mr. Fitch went out and bought himself a toupee and some testosterone additive. When I last saw them, Mrs. Fitch appeared radiant and Mr. Fitch bragged they'd had intercourse seven times in one week. Mrs. Fitch is 57 and Mr. Fitch is 72. They have been married for thirty years.

Adam Phillips, the psychoanalyst, says symptoms are unconscious constraints on possibility. I wonder if the compulsion to write this down is a way of constraining my potential to be a rocket scientist or a cliff diver or a Latina lover. Wow—I could be pretty sick. But I am tired of Mr. Phillips—his cactus nose, which is shown, along with the rest of his pensive face, on the dust jacket of his book, is beginning to disintegrate. So why not keep moving, pick another shelf. I am glad all the women's literature books got separated: *The Madwoman in the Attic, Seduction and Betrayal, Toward a Recognition of Androgyny.* Dangerous stuff. Still, they all wound up only a dictionary's width apart from one another. Listen, girls, would you please spread out a little farther so we can do our jumping jacks?

It has been six days since the thunderstorm, and *The Bastrop Advertiser* is only now reporting the damage. It can't help it, it's bi-weekly. Today's front page carries the story of a fire that started when lightning hit a tall pine tree, jumped across a road, knocked a hole in a storage building and ignited a tank of gasoline inside. Several cans of paint remained intact because, the fire chief explained, "The paint was latex so it didn't explode, but the lightning knocked the tops off all the cans. It was a pretty impressive sight."

I smile and picture dozens of bright metal paint cans, lined up proud as military officers, their thin pail handles turned down in identical Us at their sides, at ease. Zeus or Pelé or Jesus Christ points a finger and zaps the row, and the can lids pop straight up and zoom around like Frisbees, careening in the stale air of the storage room, caroming off the rotting rafters. I realize that, for the moment, I am as delighted with a small town newspaper as John Cage was with American cheese.

And after that?

Someone I read recently—to hell with attributions—said human beings are self-surprising creatures. I can go along with that. A tree fell in my own woods and I did not hear it because I, a television hater, was watching television, and now my fussy white blouse is permanently stained with marinara sauce and my hysterical colleague respects me. Best of all, my books are engaging in a series of long overdue snits, except for Cage, who thinks they are all very amusing, and I intend now to leave the prickly volumes to their nattering and take Kiri and Jake for a walk. Then I might eat an entire pound of chocolate or pick up a cowboy or fly to Italy, or possibly, just finish my work, soak in the tub and see what happens. I don't know.

REACHING FOR THE END OF TIME

1971–2005

I first encountered Olivier Messiaen's *Quartet for the End of Time* in 1971, in the basement of Florida State University's music library, where I was employed as a work-study student. The folio had languished on a low, dusty shelf for years, never checked out, and I, a scavenger delighting in all things offbeat and obscure, pounced on the composition. The *Quartet* was scored for violin, cello, piano and clarinet—my instrument. Here, I naively thought, was a piece no one else knew! Leafing through it, I noticed Messiaen's fervent dedication: "in homage to the Angel of the Apocalypse, who raises a hand toward heaven saying: 'There shall be time no longer'" and saw that the third movement, *Abyss of the Birds*, was written for solo clarinet. No matter how it sounded—I was no score reader, then—I had to be part of this ambitious work.

To start, I would perform the solo movement alone on a recital, bringing the "lost" quartet to light. I took the music to my clarinet professor, a pedagogue and technician who with one glance pronounced it negligible. I would have to negotiate the *Abyss's* odd rhythms, rackety birdcalls and excruciatingly long-held tones (like "Oms" that grow louder and louder) by myself. A composer on the faculty helped me find the single available recording of the *Quartet*, and in the music library, I listened through enormous headphones to the entire 'wondrous strange' piece over and over, moved by its spiritual vigor, a quality no other contemporary music in my experience offered. The severe leaps within its stretching lines were the antithesis of chant, and yet, they *were* chant. The quick turns between dour, weighty statements and bold, flashy warblings might have mocked ritual, and yet, they were as keenly calculated as the pairing of the stern sermon and the joyful hymn that follows. With the intensity of an evangelist, I took up my clarinet and began to practice. But by the time I had rehearsed *Abyss of the Birds* well enough to try it in public, my pride in ferreting out the music had slunk away. The solo required more physical stamina than I'd thought possible, and I was afraid that under pressure, I'd crater on it, which I did, in the very last measure, the final flourish. Instead of piping a waterfall of song, I produced one long, desperate squawk.

Thus began a pilgrimage that continues, in all of its uncertainty, today.

At the time I found Messiaen, Florida State's campus was roiling with political demonstrations, a growing drug culture, "free love," and other expressions of rebellion that marked the late '60s and early '70s. Other than a memorial march for the victims of the Kent State shootings, and a few experiments with marijuana, I was not part of that scene. I remember well the night of the first "streaking" on Landis Green. A violist friend, her violinist fiancé, and my boyfriend, a pianist, had to concede that watching more adventurous students race naked in front of the library was worth setting aside scale practice for one hour, and the four of us met at the appointed time in the safe shadow of a giant oak at the edge of the Green. I could never have torn off my clothes as one co-ed did in order to be chased by an entire fraternity, and the lily-white blind boy who galloped into the Green's fountain with no accessory but a cane took my breath away: how could he do that if he didn't know what he looked like? Yet the desire for a fresh way of regarding the world lived in us cloistered music students just as surely as it lived in those who engaged in public defiance of "the system." For me, art music, and particularly *The Quartet for the End of Time*, with its deeply spiritual impulse and wild combination of musical materials, satisfied my needs for both a meditative foundation and a radical mode of expression. I may have faltered miserably in the first performance, but *Abyss of the Birds* would help me develop a solo voice I yearned for.

In taking on *Abyss of the Birds*, I thought I was breaking ground, and maybe in the hinterlands of north Florida, I was. Little did I know that everywhere else, other musicians of my generation were unearthing the work. One year after I struck gold in the music library, the maverick Marlboro Music Festival ensemble Tashi—clarinetist Richard Stoltzman, violinist Ida Kavafian, cellist Fred Sherry and pianist Peter Serkin, the first nationally-known chamber group to perform in hippie garb—made a recording of the *Quartet* which for many listeners remains the standard, though other excellent ensembles have recorded the work since. The spiritual depth and technical challenges of the *Quartet* attracted many musical children of that time who sought strong contemporary statements and performance occasions to which they might rise. The *Quartet* is a monumental statement: with eight movements and a running time of nearly one hour, it is one of the longest pieces of chamber music in the repertoire.

After leaving Florida I vowed to perform the entire *Quartet*, and would not wait for opportunities, but create them.

The first took place at the University of Michigan, where I was a graduate student. My compatriots and I were guided by the venerable vocal coach Eugene Bossart, who told me had always wanted to learn the *Quartet*, and the results, heard in a modest recital hall, were astonishingly lyrical—an argument for the teaching of instrumentalists by experts on the human voice. Two years later, when teaching at Loyola University in New Orleans, I assembled a faculty group to play the *Quartet* in a Catholic church on St. Charles Avenue. I remember the Sunday afternoon sunlight flickering and flaring through the stained glass windows, and the feeling that Messiaen himself might be listening from a back pew, pondering his Creator. The third performance was given in Austin, Texas, in 1983, soon after I moved there, in the opera theatre at the University of Texas, with faculty from that music department. It was the only performance of the three offered on a proscenium stage, and although it went well, we were too far away from the audience, a predicament borne by many chamber musicians obliged to play in large venues. Light, close scoring calls for, and deserves, an intimate space where all communicants can share equally. I reveled in the close-knit ensemble, but missed the full intensity of our listeners.

Each of these performances took many hours of rehearsal time, because the work demands formidable technique of the players. For example, the swift sixth movement, *Dance of Fury, for the Seven Trumpets*, is completely unison, requiring precise intonation. To adjust pitch, the violinist or cellist must quickly, instinctively, roll or slide a finger of the left hand ever so slightly, infinitesimally, up or down the active string on the neck of the instrument. The clarinetist will add or subtract pressure of the lips on the mouthpiece, choose an alternate fingering, or even lower some fingers closer to inactive holes, which dulls the timbre and might not so much flatten the pitch as darken it—an illusion. No matter which instrument one is playing, the finely calibrated ear drives the physical response. The *Dance of Fury* is also unmetered, with varying time values from bar to bar, so players must rapidly and internally count the 16th-note subdivisions in diamond-cut accord, even as they achieve a flexible, mellifluous sweep. As with so many beautiful works, both exactness and unpredictability underpin the ethereal.

There are other technical challenges in the *Quartet*. The clarinet and strings are often required to play in the extreme high register, which, even among virtuosos, can be maddeningly precarious. Dynamics run from barely discernable sound to blazing loud. And the number of sustained single pitches, like tightly strung, oscillating filaments, also tax the players, even the pianist, who must dedicate the entire upper body and a well-timed pedal in service to the long, tenacious line.

Every generation spawns composers who write music that pushes previously held limits, and which traditionalists pronounce unplayable. In post-war Paris, one of those composers was Messiaen.

Olivier Messien wrote the *Quartet for the End of Time* during the winter of 1940–41, while incarcerated in Stalag VIII A, near the village of Görlitz, in the Silesian mountain region known today as Poland. The story goes that the young composer managed to make off with a pencil and some music paper, and hid out in the latrines at night, writing secretly, furiously, the piece later regarded as the finest chamber work produced during wartime imprisonment. With special permission from German authorities, he premiered the *Quartet* with three other musicians who had landed in the camp. A crowd of prisoners, many of them badly wounded and borne to the hall on stretchers, made up the audience. This scenario alone might explain why Vietnam era musicians embraced the work and brought it to the attention of American audiences. However, the *Quartet for the End of Time* did not represent Messiaen's wish for an end to personal incarceration and World War II. It was, he explained, a sustained meditation on the Book of Revelation—a hymn to eternity.

Olivier Messiaen is one of the few major twentieth century composers whose output was openly, uncompromisingly inspired by his religious faith. The only child of the Shakespeare scholar Pierre Messiaen and the poet Cécile Sauvage, who composed a book of poems titled *The Flowering Soul* while pregnant with her son, Messiaen taught himself to play the piano and at age 11 wrote his first piece, a work for piano titled *The Lady of Shalott*, based on the poem by Tennyson. Contact with Debussy's colorful, impressionistic opera *Pelléas and Melisande* made a lasting impact on the boy—it was a formal model for his own opera—but Messiaen was, from the very start, it seems, dedicated, like no other composer of his time, to expressing his Catholic faith. Here is an oft-quoted excerpt from his personal manifesto:

> *The emotion and sincerity of the work.*
> *Which shall be at the service of the dogmas of Catholic theology.*
> *The subject theological? The best, for it comprises all subjects.*
> *And the abundance of technical means allows the heart to expand freely.*

Messiaen's musical language is among the most distinctive of the 20th century. The composer was intrigued by nature, particularly birds; he was a devoted amateur ornithologist who roamed the French countryside with a tape recorder, collecting bird songs he later transcribed and used in his music. Messiaen was also a splendid instrumental colorist, having been blessed with vivid color-sound associations, the condition called synaesthesia—any sound he heard immediately produced a color in his mind's eye, and vice-versa. And so the fresh combinations of instruments he employed yielded other-worldly timbres evocative of the stained glass windows in La Trinité, the Paris cathedral he served as organist for more than 40 years. "During my captivity," he said, "it was coloured dreams that gave birth to the chords and rhythms of my *Quatour*." Messiaen was engrossed by rhythm, as well. His study of Hindu music led to a lifelong preoccupation with palindrome rhythms, mirror-structures that for him were symbols of eternity because they have no defined beginning or end. Messiaen's life spanned the entire 20th century, with the exception of exactly eight years, forward and aft. He was born in 1908, and died in 1992.

After my third performance of the *Quartet*, in 1983, I suspected I might never play the work again. Messiaen's masterpiece, for all its beauty and meaning, had produced carpal tunnel pain in my right wrist and a temporary loss of control in the fourth and fifth fingers. Repetitive motion injuries are common among today's musicians, who rehearse for technical precision to a much higher degree than did our predecessors fifty and more years ago. In the early 1980s, when my problems began, only a few doctors focused on the medical concerns of musicians; today, musician health is a legitimate specialty.

As I gained some relief through cortisone shots and

chiropractic adjustments, I gradually accepted the challenge of keeping my hands nimble enough to perform works less taxing than the *Quartet*. That left a lot of repertory; still, the loss of the *Quartet* would foreshadow the eventual loss of my life as a vibrant performer. Any musician will tell you there is no substitute for music-making at physical peak, when the body, mind, and spirit are equally, consummately engaged. Performing is who you *are*, and where God *is*.

Now I was past peak and had to figure out how to alter the conventional arc, pitch a tent close to the apex, by recapturing and maintaining the passion the *Quartet* engendered. I could do this, I thought, by listening to Messiaen's music. If I entered others' performances passionately as auditor, I might reconnect with what Messiaen must have had when he wrote the *Quartet:* a direct line to a spiritual power. Such intensity would be difficult to achieve by way of recordings. I would have to place myself as close as possible to the music-making, listening only to live performances, to which I would travel.

My notion of multiple pilgrimages was realistic, because concerts of Messiaen's music were hard to come by. I would have to leave central Texas to catch the best ones. Two exhilarating evenings stand out in my memory: an organ recital by the late composer-organist William Albright, in Dallas, and a concert in Boston featuring the *Turangalîla Symphony* with the Boston Symphony, led by Seiji Ozawa. In both, Messiaen's interpreters achieved such perfect symbiosis between composer, performers and listeners I might as well have been on stage, playing my clarinet. Time stopped.

As my travels proceeded and my knowledge of Messiaen

grew, it occurred to me to ingest all of the religious symbols and technical devices behind the music. I should do this, I thought, because it would put me inside the composer's head, surely the source of the intensity I wished to recover. But each time I approached the music this way, I felt stymied by Messiaen's overwhelmingly Catholic "program," and retreated. I couldn't force myself to go this route; mine was a quest of the heart and body, not the intellect. Besides, I was the last person to plunge into what I saw as a theological swamp. My spiritual life hadn't been formally linked to a religion since childhood church attendance, which was mostly benign Methodist (my father's brand), except when my mother, raised Unitarian, switched us over to a Presbyterian church for a time, and then an Episcopal one, because the pastors for those congregations wrote better sermons. Having a deep-seated aversion to anything resembling a club, I've never as an adult wanted to articulate a faith or join an organized religion. The first activity would devalue an inner experience—to describe in words would limit it—and the second, which seems to me to be based on fear and tribalism, closes off possibilities.

    Still, I have always dabbled in religious matters, which might make me a sort of aspirant, implying upward movement toward some sort of triumph. But I am continually quashing the vertical impulse and reacting to it in others. I want the Shaker hymn *Simple Gifts*, not the Protestant battle anthem *Onward Christian Soldiers*. There was a time in my 30s, not long after the third *Quartet* performance, when Pope John Paul passed through San Antonio, and the idea of a pope, a king of a religion, struck me as so preposterous that I cultivated a collection of Pope memorabilia as a local corrective. Friends aware of my delight in pontiff kitsch made me gifts of Pope paper dolls, Pope snow globes, Pope soap-on-a-rope. My most prized possession was a signed and numbered Pope lawn sprinkler: a three-foot replica of John Paul, painted on plywood, fitted on the back with a hose connector and some plastic tubing. When hooked up to a hose, the Pope's hands spouted water. The sprinkler's official name was "Let Us Spray," and it was the envy of my unchurched friends, as well as many of the churched ones. One morning, I found it missing from my garden, and though I was angry about the theft, I joked that God was not amused by my irreverence and had seen fit to cast out my graven image. The next time I moved, I carried the rest of my Pope trumpery to the Salvation Army. Presumably it was divided into piles headed for Toys and Housewares, and even Women's Clothing, where an "I Prayed With the Pope" t-shirt from Denver, featuring the pontiff surrounded by a pestilence of prairie dogs, was snatched up, I hope, by someone with a sense of humor.

While I was traveling to hear Messiaen and chuckling over the Pope, the daily newspaper in Austin hired me as music critic, beginning an accidental writing career. Even so, I continued to perform in chamber groups and the city opera orchestra with the help of chiropractors, yoga instructors and a gifted Rolfer whose manipulations increased my height by half an inch. Working with both music and words was often frustrating. I found that I couldn't practice the clarinet, put down the instrument, and immediately take up the pen. There had to be a transitional hour between the use of each language, during which I would perform a household task such as baking bread or gardening. In shuttling back and forth from one to the other, I experienced a physical sensation, a light-headedness. A neuroscientist could explain exactly why this was so; put simply, verbal and musical language centers reside in different parts of the brain. I felt a slight, but real chemical switch.

Eventually, though, words achieved a solid, practical purchase on my life. I returned to school for a degree in writing, and then, sixteen years after my final performance of the *Quartet*, I resigned from my last ongoing chamber group and moved to Ithaca, New York for a post-doc in writing at Cornell. I embraced a hermetic existence there, retreating to my rented cottage after school, listening not to Messiaen, but to recordings of the late Beethoven quartets, as if confirming my musical dotage.

But Messiaen returned to me, upstaging Beethoven, when a Cornell faculty group invited me to take the second clarinet part in a performance of his splashy, fluttery *Oiseaux Exotiques* for piano and small orchestra. By then I played so seldom it would take two months of rigorous daily practice to execute my part in a professional manner. And, whether or not I was practicing, the carpal tunnel pain in my right wrist now woke me up at night, spasming up my arm, into my shoulder and neck. One of the doctors I consulted identified mild scoliosis, a structural imbalance that at middle age was affecting more than that wrist; all of my limbs were vulnerable.

Yet I eagerly accepted the invitation to perform *Oiseaux Exotiques*. It was a gift I hadn't expected: a last chance, a coda. And with that commitment in hand, I took on another: a two-month bird-watching course offered by Cornell's renowned ornithology department. My motivation had nothing to do with Messiaen, I thought. I simply wanted to take advantage of a fine program that would force me to get out of the house on Saturday mornings.

The Messiaen concert thrilled me—how could it not,

since my job was to plant myself within an ecstatic sound-tapestry, chirping and shrieking the calls of the wood thrush, the lark, and even the prairie chicken? *Oiseaux Exotiques* contains the songs of forty-six birds from India, China, Malaysia, the Canary Islands, South America and North America, including the Chinese liothrix, four different vireos, and a vivacious little singer Messiaen calls the Carolina troglodyte, commonly known as the Carolina wren. Within this aviary, the pain in my wrist, arm, shoulder and back temporarily evaporated, and I walked off the stage and into the night, glowing. The next morning, in the cold spring rain, I gulped extra-strength Tylenol and drove one-handed with thirty other aspiring bird-watchers to the Montezuma National Wildlife Refuge near Seneca Falls, where transient Canada geese, mallards and dozens of other waterfowl species clogged the marshes, looking to me misplaced and confused. I remember envying the sharp-sighted engineering major who later that day spotted a female ruby-crowned kinglet flitting among the branches of an evergreen thicket. The female bears no red cap; she looks like any number of what our instructor called LBJs, or Little Brown Jobs. How could that young man possibly distinguish her, I wondered. She wasn't even singing.

At the end of that year, I moved to the desolate reach of Wyoming to write, and eventually to teach writing and music history at the state university in Laramie. I was lonely there, and resumed my Messiaen excursions, fixating first on the composer's only American commission, a piece for solo piano, horn, xylorimba, glockenspiel and orchestra, titled *From the Canyons to the Stars*. For this project, Messiaen was determined to find inspiration in the American landscape, and in 1971, lured by a photograph of Bryce Canyon, he bought a plane ticket to Salt Lake City and spent a month in southern Utah, visiting Bryce Canyon, Cedar Breaks and Zion National Parks. The result was a gloriously excessive work of twelve movements that takes an hour and a half to play.

Knowing I was not likely ever to hear a live performance of *Canyons*, I found the only recording in print, loaded it into my car's CD player, and on one bright weekend in May, the same time of year that Messiaen went west, drove over to Utah to hike Bryce and listen to the same birds Messiaen would have heard exactly thirty years before. I knew my desire to retrace his steps was impure—a greed for someone else's transcendence—but set it aside, for I had come to realize that moving my body through space, by way of motorized vehicles or my two feet, had become a partial substitute for the physical intensity of music. I'd completed my transformation from music-maker to witness, relinquishing musical notes, instrument and stage for words, pens, and geography. I *had* to do this.

I had made a list of Messiaen's Utah birds, whose songs I had learned from a CD of bird-calls acquired at Cornell. I had brought binoculars and a camera, too. But on the morning I walked the dry red path among the luminous pink spires and hoodoos carved by centuries of wind, rain and snow, I heard and saw nothing that had anything to do with birds. Had Bryce's environment changed that much in 25 years, or had I simply missed the dawn chorus? Once, I spotted a small specimen on a branch of one of the gnarly pines bunched here and there on the canyon floor, but it didn't sing, and didn't even fly when I came close. It might as well have been a decoy.

I turned on my booted heel and started up Wall Street, a dark, damp trail that ran between two mammoth bulwarks of stone so high and close together there was but a slice of light at the top, where the two walls nearly met. The sounds of my boots, heel-toe, heel-toe, bounced off the rock dryly, like castanets. I stopped to listen to the echo, and in that moment an elderly couple appeared at the other end of the tipped walls, and seeing me, paused. Then they began to speak softly, and their words did not ricochet off the stone edifices, but rather wafted down to me like feathers. They were French.

The woman turned back to rest, but the man continued toward me, to explore the length of the path. As he approached, I greeted him, "Bonjour," and his face brightened as he responded at length in his language.

This was the Frenchman's first visit to the United States, he said. He and his wife had heard of Bryce's beauty, and wanted to be sure to see it. I confessed I was there to retrace the steps of his countryman, Olivier Messiaen.

"Why do you want to do this?" he asked.

"I want to hear what he heard," I answered.

"And that is . . . "

"Birds," I said. "But all I hear today is the wind."

"Perhaps what you hear is enough," said the Frenchman.

A year later, the San Francisco Opera mounted Messiaen's only stage work, based on the life of St. Francis of Assisi. It would be the first American (and only third ever) production of *St. François*, and I flew over for the weekend to witness it—the complicated travel to and from Laramie taking longer than the time I actually spent in the city. The opera, a series of tableaux dramatizing significant events in St. Francis's life, started at 6:30 PM and ended close to midnight, and required an orchestra so large and varied that wide stage extensions had to be built, eliminating several rows of seats in front. From my perch in the first balcony, I gazed down on what looked like a giant painting of musical hell by Hieronymous Bosch, jammed to the edges with musicians curled around one another, instruments wedged into adjacent armpits or pressed into stomachs. In contrast, when the curtain lifted, I saw a striking, minimal set by Hans Dieter Schaal in shades of gray, with thick moveable walls, and a raised walkway that curved back to infinity. Hovering over this was an immense round ball: the sun, the moon, an egg, a soul? Together, these represented a monastery, its rooms, its garden, and all that existed within them. With the exception of the Angel, who appeared in bluebird blue, St. Francis and his brothers were clad in neutral colors. Messiaen's aural reds and greens, purples and oranges, made up the rest of the spectrum.

    The work proceeds with deliberate majesty. A few listeners in my balcony row grew audibly impatient; our seats in the venerable old opera house were tight, and one had the choice only of sitting straight up or squinching forward, elbows or forearms on knees: the house-side version of the arrangement in the pit. As much as I loved Messiaen's music, I began to wonder if I'd flown all that way to witness a dud. And then came—at precisely the right place in the opera, in the evening—the scene where St. Francis, after a prolonged, agonizing build-up, reaches out with one hand to touch, and finally embrace, a leper, risking his life to pass the love of God directly to the decaying man, flesh upon flesh. I could not hold back the sudden tears; the impact of the *Quartet* had returned to me.

    Yet after returning to Wyoming I embarked on a head-trip, snatching up the Catholic authors Messiaen revered, as if by reading I could sustain the effect of St. Francis's touch. I found

Hans Urs von Balthasar's *Heart of the World*—beautiful, but not as accessible as I'd hoped—and tried to connect with Paul Claudel's poems and his commentary *A Poet Before the Cross*, which I tossed aside after the first chapter. Nothing there for me. Finally, I re-read the Book of Revelation—the inspiration for the *Quartet*—and some recent interpretations of it, and at last realized how wildly mutable and kaleidoscopic Revelation is. An angel with a rainbow crown and clothing of clouds, one foot in the sea and one on earth? Why, no wonder "godless" musicians of the Vietnam era latched on to the *Quartet*. Revelation was the ultimate trip, complete with symbols one could contemplate long after the drug of the moment—be it chemical, material, or what Karen Armstrong calls a "bad religion" (one that stifles "the individual's search for transcendent meaning and the absolute truth beyond ego")—wears off. Like music, it can be variously perceived, and I began to regard Revelation as a grand, hallucinogenic painting, kin to Messiaen's orchestra for *St. François*, not holy writ ossified by tradition. Here was a section of the New Testament I could view as more than a historical myth toward living a right life. It was wild, hairy literature; it was, as Messiaen knew, a basis for art.

  I put away my books and forgot about Messiaen until a faculty ensemble at the University of Wyoming, planning a performance of the *Quartet for the End of Time* in response to the Iraq war, asked me to speak at the concert. One of them had spotted me marching in an anti-war demonstration in front of Laramie's snow-covered courthouse. The Iraq war was not as unpopular in Laramie as Vietnam had been in Tallahassee; for every passerby who waved in support of our peace march, another gave us the finger. At the *Quartet* performance, I offered a description of the *Quartet's* premiere, stressing Messiaen's heroic feat, making art under extreme conditions. Then my colleagues began to play, and I yearned to be the clarinetist, to help sing Messiaen's sorrowful, joyous, mysterious songs. But it could never happen, not now. Although my right wrist had been surgically healed of carpal tunnel syndrome, the pinkie of the same hand resembled a fattened sausage link, slightly bent. My body had generated a new, more unusual hand ailment, Dupuytrens Contracture, a thickening of fascia along the tendons in the palm and fingers. During the *Abyss of the Birds*, the crimped finger twitched, a broken wing.

Not long after the concert I happened upon the last book I would ever read about Messiaen. *For the End of Time: The Story of the Messiaen Quartet*, had just been published by Rebecca Rischin, a clarinetist who traveled to France to hunt down the details of the quartet's composition in Stalag VIII A. I was shocked to learn that after the war, the composer developed a simplified story (the one I had known and passed on) of the quartet's genesis, glorifying himself at the expense of others, flattening the fascinating facts, obscuring his compositional process and magnifying his suffering and the loathsome conditions under which he worked. His wife, Yvonne Loriod, who had been his student and frequently performed his work, tended his musical legacy after his death and further embroidered the tale. Until Rischin made the effort to interview musicians and others who were in the camp, musicologists accepted Messiaen's exaggerations as gospel.

The long-held myth says that Messiaen composed the entire quartet within the walls of Stalag VIII A, when in fact, he wrote *Abyss of the Birds* earlier, when he was stationed as a medical orderly at Verdun. There, he met the cellist Etienne Pasquier and clarinetist Henri Akoka, who played together in a military orchestra, and, inspired by Akoka's style and the birds in the area, Messiaen composed the clarinet solo with no thought of a larger work. Then the Germans roared in, and the three musicians were captured. Akoka managed to take his clarinet on the ensuing forty-three-mile march to an encampment near Nancy, and while waiting to be sent to Stalag VIII A, he sight-read *Abyss of the Birds* for Messiaen. Pasquier, who had been obliged to leave his cello in Verdun, held the music for him.

Messiaen also claimed the fourth movement, *Interlude*, was the first movement he wrote, although it could have been the first he composed in Stalag VIII A, for it is scored only for violin, clarinet, and cello. (Violinist Jean Le Boulaire joined the group in the camp, and Pasquier was given a cello there. The piano was made available later.) Additionally, the fifth movement, *Praise to the Eternity of Jesus* and the eighth, *Praise to the Immortality of Jesus*, respectively for cello with piano, and violin with piano, were not lightning bolts from the clouds over Görlitz, but refashionings of pieces Messiaen had written before the war. Cannibalizing or building upon previous work is common among composers and other creators—after all, many believe God cobbled us together from earlier projects, such as clay. It seemed odd that Messiaen would deny this practice.

More importantly, there is the tale, kept vividly alive by his wife, of Messiaen sneaking into the camp latrines to compose. Those who were there told it differently. Early on, Messiaen was recognized as a famous composer, relieved of physical labor, and given the materials and privacy to write music. "What I know is that we were not allowed to disturb him," Pasquier told Rischin.

Pasquier himself was relieved of work in a granite quarry

and assigned a job as camp cook, once he was identified as a famous cellist. Le Boulaire and Akoka fared well, too. Anyone familiar with accounts of concentration camp orchestras knows the Reich sometimes protected musicians, providing them instruments, music, rehearsal time, and, in the context of horrible deprivation, relatively easy labor. Many accounts cite one key German—a music-lover or secret humanist—who served as intermediary or protector for musicians. In Messiaen's case, it was an officer named Karl-Albert Brüll, who spoke fluent French and whose father was president of the Catholic Youth of Silesia. He was also sympathetic to the Jews. But despite Brüll's extraordinary assistance to Messiaen, the composer failed to acknowledge him publicly until 1991.

A long time ago I must have decided that anyone who creates great art must be an admirable person. It was a naïve assumption, or perhaps it was a desire. I wanted the whole package to be perfect, one part a reflection of the other. In wishing this, I succumbed to the vertical impulse, building an exceedingly high pedestal for Olivier Messiaen. Down he crashed, and one day, on a hike in Wyoming's Snowy Range, I found myself, after all those years, talking to him. Why did you lie about the composition of the *Quartet*? Why did you deny Brüll?

Rischin offered possible answers regarding the composing process, politely speculating that Messiaen was motivated by practicality, pedagogy, and kindness. He wanted to make the story simple for students, scholars and the press, paring the analytical details of the work, citing the modest fourth movement as the first one composed, even though it meant obliterating the histories of the phenomenal solo movements (the third, fifth, and eighth). "From a compositional standpoint, Rischin wrote, "a less complex and less ambitious movement might serve as a starting point—the prelude to rather than an interlude for—a much greater composition." No matter the sequence of composition, she added, Messiaen might have decided on three solo movements to give his compatriots equal roles in the birth of the work. But however it happened, Rischin concluded the composer wanted to "leave no doubt that he intended a quartet all along."

"His omissions serve[d] to preserve the myths surrounding the piece and the mystery surrounding the man," she wrote.

And Karl-Albert Brüll? Having known a number of image-conscious composers, I began to see how Messiaen and his wife might have wished to impress the public with his brilliance and devotion to art, dramatizing his ability to create heaven-inspired work against the most horrifying odds. Acknowledging Brüll, the real hero of the day, would have blown the Messiaens' miraculous story, revealing an iconoclastic composer to be a mere human being who depended upon, and then selfishly disclaimed, a daring generosity that, like St. Francis's, transcended doctrine. I will probably never know the full truth—no doubt there are facts and nuances waiting for the next researcher—but the truth Rischin uncovered for me was the image of a gangly fellow in a beret working brilliantly the levers and pulleys of his art and craft, to the glory of something greater than himself, yet not without the pretensions artists attempt and often fail to erase. Messaien's connection to God came not from something he owned, but something he could only yearn for, and in that sense, he was no different from the rest of us.

My relationship with Messiaen is not over; at the very least, it is teaching me I can't get out of living with contradictions.

Last year I consulted a hand specialist who advised surgery for my Dupuytrens. The thickening in the right little finger had increased and dropped down into the palm, between the fourth and fifth fingers—the typical starting point for the affliction before it worms its way across the hand. This was the location of my initial carpal tunnel symptom; the insidious groundwork had been laid since the first performance of the *Quartet*.

I put off the surgery, hoping the disease might stall, until one cold day, when I spilled the contents of my change purse onto the floor of the Laramie K-Mart and had to accept the help of a small child to retrieve the coins. How essential the littlest digit is to the most ordinary tasks, such as picking up a dime between the thumb and forefinger. Without their fellows in concert, the big guys are clumsy, inflexible.

To remove Dupuytrens tissue, a surgeon can't simply slice straight down the center of the finger. A to B would deny access to the thickening that has crept into pockets along the sides, and would leave an inflexible scar. The most desirable incision zigzags crazily across the finger and palm. Afterward, the patient embarks on weeks of physical therapy to regain something close to normal functioning. One day, I asked my therapist if I could do more at home than repeat my finger exercises and squeeze clay.

"Did you say you were a clarinetist?" she asked.

"Yes," I said.

"The best thing you can do is play your instrument. Practice the piece you love most."

I stared at this strong, ruddy woman, whose clientele consisted mostly of daredevils: bronco-busters, downhill skiers, mountain climbers. What could she possibly know about musicians?

Then I thought of the *Abyss*. "I haven't played it in twenty-two years," I said. "My fingers won't work right. I'll sound terrible."

"But you love it. Do it. Trust me," she said.

❦ LOVE FROM AFAR ❦

1991–2005

For my fortieth birthday, my second husband gave me a talking doll called The Ideal Man. The Ideal Man was a foot tall and dressed in regatta garb: boat shoes, khakis, white shirt and navy blazer. His hair was chestnut and tousled just so. He had blue eyes, a straight nose, and when one pressed his stomach, his voice box, articulated to sound like President John F. Kennedy, spoke from the following program: "You look wonderful." "How 'bout a nice, long massage." "Here's a glass of wine, I'll light a fire."

My husband and I laughed and laughed at The Ideal Man; I believe he hoped its patter would lighten the aftermath of a shipwreck we wouldn't survive. We demonstrated The Ideal Man for our neighbors in Austin, passing him around at parties, turning his phrases into cocktail operettas. "Here's a glass of wine . . . " my husband would croon, conspiratorially. "I'll light a fire," I'd pipe, with a naughty wink.

Lightening up, though helpful at times, can serve to distance important conversations of the heart, and when I realized that was mostly what The Ideal Man was good for, I stashed him in a basket of odds and ends and forgot about him. Nine years later, having left our riverside home in Texas and relocated to teach music history and writing in high, dry Wyoming, I was surprised to find The Ideal Man in a box hastily packed by the moving company. "Oh, you Silly," I said, lifting him from a knot of old bathing suits, remembering with fondness my former husband's sense of humor. For after all, there were some parts of our life together I missed—pleasures enjoyed early in our marriage, such as travel, entertaining, pride in our home. But that was then, this was now. I set The Ideal Man aside, intending to truck him down to the Laramie Goodwill on top of the mountain of belongings I no longer needed. Yet when time came to make the trip, I plucked him from the heap and perched him on the new futon.

I spent three years trying to give up The Ideal Man. In the first year I hauled him out for guests so often that his voice box, already weak, finally broke. A male friend undressed him and poked around his back, trying to get at the battery that surely powered him, but could find none. "Ha-ha! So The Ideal Man can't talk!" shouted the wife of the fellow who tried to repair him. I wasn't laughing, though; I found myself inexplicably wishing to swat the woman for making fun of my defenseless doll. The Ideal Man never looked the same after that; his perfect costume, once disassembled, fit badly. Poor Ideal Man. Now I *had* to keep him.

I changed rental houses in Laramie twice more, and with each move, and each spring-cleaning between, tried and failed to bid farewell to The Ideal Man. More than once he rode to Goodwill, and rode back. More than once he made it to the curb and was snatched to safety as the garbage truck approached. I began to suspect it would take a really rotten mood to send him packing, and I rarely fell into one; for all the adjustments I'd had to make, I was happier and more content than I'd been in a long time. Finally, one dark winter day, I willed myself to get rid of The Ideal Man, calling myself a baby for hanging onto him so long. Even now I resist saying how I did it, for to remember makes me sad. I drank a glass of wine, turned up my *Joan Sutherland: Mad Scenes* CD full blast, and thrust him deep into the trash.

Thus it was that in the middle of my third snowbound, wind-blows-your-head-off winter in Laramie, a small college community where a single woman professor's social life consists of potlucks for department job candidates and holiday suppers where the hosts feel compelled to pair her with the same available man, I signed up with an internet dating service, one promising to match clients with potential "soul-mates," a love marketing term that to me has always implied a creepy symbiosis like that of Mimi and Rudolfo in *La Boheme*. But what the heck. I requested a field of choices as far away as Colorado Springs—180 miles south of Laramie and 2500 feet lower—and the selected suitors and I auditioned each other by email and phone.

I stuck with the scene long enough for single dates with three Colorado men, the first a fellow who ran a shooting sports complex. As a woman given to rescuing injured birds, rabbits and dogs, I had no idea what that is—but I do now. It's a country place acres and acres big, to which hunting enthusiasts flock on the weekends to shoot clay pigeons and real ones. This man professed to being an avid reader, but when he pulled up in front of the university fine arts building in a white pick-up with a toolbox in the back, and wearing a cowboy hat that surely would have had docking privileges, were we anywhere close to water, I suspected we'd be working from diametrically opposed scripts. My energy was high at that moment; I had just given a lecture on

John Cage, and cajoled my music history class into performing a five-part aleatoric composition, noisy and fun. I couldn't begin to explain this to the shooting sportsman, and I'm sure he found me equally boring, as, over a plate of hamburger tacos, I listened quietly to his tales of horse breeding.

Next, I heard from an engineer who on the phone sounded overly solicitous, but decent. I agreed to meet him for lunch, but over the course of our conversations I had detected gaps in his life story and on a hunch before our date, Googled him and found a photograph of the fellow in his freshman class at a technical institute, ca. 1962. He had billed himself as 50 years old, but in fact, a simple calculation indicated he was 60, and when we met I saw I was correct. A friend wondered why I didn't confront the engineer about his lie. But what would be the point? I turned down his next invitation with the valid excuse that I was exiting the region for the summer.

The third date was a university administrator, a man several inches shorter than advertised who made a show of his silver Lexus in the parking lot of the hushed, candlelit restaurant where he insisted we meet. At dinner he avoided conversation by flagging the waiter constantly to request fresh napkins, more cream, or extra spoons, and without asking me ordered the most pretentious dessert on the menu: a pair of enormous chocolate bombas soused with brandy and lit tableside. Afterward I made the mistake of stopping by his house for a nightcap, during which a snowstorm moved into the Front Range, rendering the roads impassable. I had no choice but to spend the night, but as it turned out, my host was harmless. After a kiss and a hug, he put me to bed in his guest room, went out, and reappeared in his skivvies with two paperback books, one for each of us. Then he snapped on two nightlights, climbed in beside me, and we lay there silently like an old married couple, reading until we fell asleep.

After five years in Wyoming I moved back to Texas—not to Austin, but to a university town close to Dallas. By then, my collective dating experience had taken on the qualities of an *opera seria* or an *opera buffa*, depending on my mood. The impression was undoubtedly shared by my far-flung girlfriends, whose patience on the phone had enabled me to survive five Wyoming winters. These faithful heroines offered several coaching styles. The motherly types allowed me to whine, then lectured me in stern tones to make more informed choices. Those gifted at analysis were ever ready to dissect the rat in question. The singles, or those who were particularly independent, could be counted on for spirited commiseration and cheerful commands to throw myself back into my work. To be honest, all of my girlfriends are rich combinations of the above, and may the spirits of Mozart's Pamina, Strauss's Marschallin, and Verdi's Azucena bless them for that.

One spring morning, as I was planting a patch of native Texas perennials in the yard of the first home I had bought on my own, I suddenly saw how in Wyoming I had, as my loneliness and list of dating encounters grew, increasingly *performed* my remote social life for my friends, at once fashioning the scenery, screeching the arias, and starring in the folk-dance finale. In fact, I had turned my male acquaintances into caricatures and myself into a stock character: the Perfectly Eligible Woman Who Will Never Meet Her Match. With my trowel, I scooped a deep hole, yodeled her down into the soil, and set an unassuming lantana on top.

During my Wyoming exile I traveled often to important cultural events, determined to maintain a connection to High Art despite my low-density zip code. One particular summer, I attended the premiere of Kaija Saariaho's opera *L'Amour de loin* ("Love from afar") in Santa Fe. The work is based on the story of a troubadour prince, Jaufré Rudel, who, weary of his licentious life, devotes himself to the vision of an ideal love, composing song after song to the unattainable woman. Soon enough, a Pilgrim sails up, announcing that Jaufré's ideal exists, but far away: she is Clémence, the beautiful Countess of Tripoli. Jaufré composes ever more furiously, and the Pilgrim sails back to Tripoli to spill the beans. Clémence is first annoyed by news of a distant admirer, then succumbs to the love-dream, though, as a Christian, she is compelled to obsess over her deservedness. The Pilgrim reports to Jaufré, who insists on being ferried to Tripoli. Once again, the Pilgrim launches his boat. But as the distance between the lovers closes, Jaufré and Clémence grow anxious, and Jaufré's jangled nerves crescendo to chronic illness. By the time he reaches the shores of Tripoli attired in his best velvet, he has just enough breath left to belt out, with remarkable virtuosity, a final love-duet with Clémence, who then decides the whole thing is her fault and naturally enters a convent.

In the opera's program interview, the composer said she was drawn to the tale because the main characters—the troubador who wants to express his love through writing music, and the lady who was sent to a foreign continent—were like two parts of herself. Kaija Saariaho, who is Finnish, found the artistic establishment in her country oppressive and moved to Paris to develop her compositional voice and career. A radical change of scene obviously worked for her; the opera was a big success.

I was drawn to Saariaho's story, for in a sense it mirrored

mine. It's hard to make good art when there's high drama at home; to save one's soul, one must leave, find a place more closely allied to the heart's desire. I also saw how the story driving the opera could be interpreted as a warning to artists against proximity to their material. From a certain distance, one possesses just what is necessary for good work. Get too close to the muse and it's curtains for you.

But the opera also gives us the death of idealism. How else is one to love?

Two months after *L'Amour de loin* I adopted a young male Australian Shepherd I named Cole, after Cole Porter, the songwriter. I had to fly from Laramie to Chapel Hill to get him, as there were no Australian Shepherd rescues available within a two-day drive of Wyoming. Residents of the mountain west have practical uses for herding dogs; no one out there acquires an Aussie and changes their mind when the pup insists on—and will take in some form if not given—at least three miles of hard running a day.

I knew what I was doing. Early in my second marriage I had fallen for and adopted another Aussie puppy I named after the Maori opera diva Kiri Te Kanawa, and finally gave my girl up to heaven when she was fifteen, a year after I became single. Kiri had been a headstrong alpha, shrewd enough to sneak quietly out of many a fenced yard—wood, metal or electric—and drive me crazy searching the neighborhood for a glimpse of her tail. On this smart, maddening dog I projected qualities I wanted for myself: intelligence, independence, self-assurance. I assumed Cole would receive the same projections, like a blank screen, but none of Ideal Kiri would stick to him. Instead, he immediately assumed the role of my protector, jealously guarding the front door, sleeping beside my bed, always coming when called and politely, expectantly, tilting his head as if to ask, "How may I serve you now?"

I would have none of Cole's attentiveness at first. Why did he hang around so much? Why was he so easy? Why was he not . . . Kiri?

And after a certain number of road trips, I found myself thinking of the men I'd dated and asking, why are none of them my former husband?

My nostalgia lasted about a week. Cole, eager, devoted, and tenacious, convinced me a low-maintenance pet is desirable, and I remembered why I had left my husband. Still, I wondered: how come this bit of wistfulness, several years post-divorce? It seemed that if I could figure this out, I'd have something to go on.

Now my Texas phone was ringing. Pat, my artist friend in Baltimore, wanted to talk. "I'm in such a funk," she said. "I don't know what to make next. I want a new project."

Pat and I had just finished collaborating with our choreographer friend Joyce on a piece combining live music, dance, spoken word, and paper sculpture. Performances in Baltimore and Ithaca had gone exceedingly well, and Pat's post-partum slump was predictable. I had somehow avoided the condition this time; I'd finally learned, for better or worse, to keep at least two projects going at once, but on different timelines, so when one is complete I have another to move to without flailing away from scratch. This is no sign of ingenuity, but of self-protection. It's like having more than one boyfriend, I guess, though I wouldn't really know.

I accepted Pat's challenge to brainstorm. "What about those drawings you were working on two summers ago?" I asked. "Or your trip to Spain—didn't that give you some ideas?" We talked and talked, and some viable notions began to emerge.

I thought I remembered doing this with my husband, who was a composer. For all the headaches and heartaches, we had both been fully engaged with our creative work, and in my memory, I saw us blurting to one another at breakfast, with no prelude, "It can't be eight chapters—it has to be ten," or "Would it be better if I cut four bars?" None of the men I'd dated could communicate with me in that way, and now I saw how, given my expectations, I had been wasting my time, and theirs.

Pat and I signed off—11 PM Texas time, midnight hers. Then I listened to the winter rain splash gently against the windows of my house. I thought of Kaija Saariaho, the composer who wanted to express love through art but had to leave home to do it. Then I admitted that despite the artistic intimacy I imagined I shared with my husband, he had, to my sorrow, not always welcomed my accomplishments and often discouraged them. I was actually making better, more adventurous work away from him.

Now there was nothing left to imagine I missed.

Were this a real opera, the heroine would bask in this clarifying moment, face radiant, arms outstretched, even as a series of high suspensions in the orchestra hints at the *denouement*: the appearance of an Ideal Man, who, finally, unsought and unbidden, walks confidently—not timid! not overbearing!—from the wings, extends his hand, and sings

Come, let us make a life together
Sail one boat, take our pleasure
and guess what, I already live in the same city . . .

But this is no opera, as I was so rudely reminded last night when Nancy, a single music professor two time zones to the west of Texas, called to report she'd just been told by a reasonably intelligent, middle-aged man, "Read all the upbeat articles you want, but the dirty little secret is that no man of our generation has ever been entirely comfortable with the idea of an equal or accomplished partner."

I asked Nancy if she believed this.

"I'm not sure," she said. "But if he's correct, I should stop hoping for the kind of relationship I want."

"Me, too," I said.

"If he can't take it, that I love what I do, with some success, then forget it," she said.

"Damn right," I said.

"What are you doing?" she asked.

"My work," I answered. "I am trying to express love."

"Really. For who?"

"For no one," I said. "But an object doesn't seem to matter. It's going pretty well."

At that moment, Cole pushed his muzzle under my elbow, reminding me it was time to get ready for bed. I said good-night to Nancy, poured a glass of wine, and, as it was a cool evening, rare in Texas, I lit a fire. "Look at me," I said to Cole. "I'm becoming my own Ideal Man."

But Cole, hard as he stared, could not understand my words, so I patted his head and sipped my wine, watching the flames flare and sway and curl.

My friend Claude, another composer, talks to me about attempting to make an ideal world, in music.

"To try and make that ideal the way that I see it, and the way I hear it, as it passes in real time, is a disappointing project in and of itself," he says. "And yet it's exciting, too, because once I get to the point where the whole piece is completed in my imagination, I can see it! I want to say, 'Well, look up here! There it is! Just play that!' But of course it doesn't work that way. As a piece becomes tangible, inevitably something is lost."

When we spoke, Claude, who lives in Indiana, was on his way to Europe for two months to compose. Last summer, I inexplicably accepted a residency in parched Wyoming to work on a book about a rainforest on the Gulf Coast, and on the way back to Texas, stopped in Santa Fe to witness another new opera, Thomas Ades's *The Tempest*, based on Shakespeare. I was glad this one was rooted in the Renaissance, not the Middle Ages, promising at least a measure of happiness. And having just descended from drought-ridden plains, I was especially interested in comparing Santa Fe's uses of water in Ades's opera to that in Saariaho's. In *Love From Afar*, Jaufré and Clemence, separated by a sea, corresponded across the depths, assisted by a match-making Pilgrim. When Jaufré made his move, it was by way of the Pilgrim's skiff, drifting across a wide pool of real water. The lovers didn't moisten so much as a toe until their tragedy was complete. But in *The Tempest*, Miranda and Ferdinand, flung from their separate vessels—and having survived full-immersion baptism, if you will—wash up on the same island; Ferdinand literally emerges from a watery shoreline at the lip of the stage, wringing wet. Yes, it is love at first sight, though the realistic storm-conjurer Prospero warns, "... this swift business I must uneasy make lest too light winning make the prize light." Ideal love in *The Tempest* begins with proximity, and the lovers, clad not in velvet but in rags, marry in secret, while enslaved spirits and territorial old men haggle center stage.

Last night I dreamed I was writing an opera with an enormous cast of characters: an ex-husband, three dates, three friends, six opera singers, two dogs, a Finnish composer, a talking doll, and a potted plant miming the role of a deaf-mute. Because I was setting scenes all over the country, the production was sure to go way over budget, and the general manager of the commissioning company was threatening to fire me.

"You think we're made of money?" she screamed. "You think this is Santa Fe? You don't have one major donor, Hon. Get a grip. Cut to the chase."

I woke up in a sweat, angry with the general manager, who spoke the truth, but in a clichéd, impolite manner, giving me an excuse to take offense and stomp away. But after two cups of espresso and a long ramble with Cole around the wide lake north of town, I returned to face the music. There I stood, alone in my living room, trying to explain to the general manager how the opera might end.

"Suddenly, this great guy . . ."

"Oh, can it," she said.

"I inherit a tropical island . . ."

"*Really,*" she said. "Think of the upkeep."

"Okay, I just practice mindfulness, give thanks for the flowers, and write in my fucking journal," I said.

"Are you crazy?" she cried. "I expect more of you. And no

more foliage. One appearance by that silly lantana was enough."

I dropped to my new beige metro-style sofa, wishing guiltily for a red velvet fainting couch.

"I give up," I said. "Nothing, no one, is an ideal wrap for this show."

"That's not my problem," the general manager said. "And guess what? I'm leaving this scene. Time to pay me for all the hard work I've put in."

I paused to hug Cole, who had heard the rising voices and trotted in to protect me. I looked the general manager straight in the eye.

"I don't owe you a dime. You commissioned this," I said.

"You proposed it," she shot back. "Now give me the leisure retirement I deserve."

"All right — done!" I shouted, furious. But then I took pause. For I didn't believe I could release my need for the general manager; specifically, for her expectations of me, without which I'd never finish another piece, nor meet a possible partner. Maybe I could bribe her to stay on a little longer.

"Listen," I said. "How about if the opera ends with you. One more act: a grand finale. Dancing, singing, whatever you want."

"No," she said. "I can't do any of those things."

"Come on," I pleaded, "You always wanted to be a star."

"Not really," said the general manager. Then she lowered her voice to a whisper. "Have you ever noticed that I have no talent? Why not let me exit gracefully? Give the last scene to your little dog."

But Cole, sensing the conflict was essentially over, had already padded over to his water dish for a few slurps—what he always does before following me, as I drag myself back to my study.

Tune up the amateur orchestra, turn on the 40-watt bulbs. And forgive me any ruined voices, miscast characters, fuzzy projections and dropped canoe paddles, as I've just been left to my own devices, and it seems I'm fresh out of them.

It's just Cole and me now, in a spare bedroom of mismatched bookshelves and cabinets, a gaudy ceiling fan installed by the previous owner wheeling lopsided over our heads. I sit down to the one good piece of furniture I've loved for 20 years—a long oak library table positioned here before the tallest window—and somehow resist the urge to jump up and straighten the pictures, file two months of receipts, or call to check on the dry cleaning.

No, I just sit at the table.

Believe me, it won't last long.

Even so, it occurs to me, this empty stage offers the chance to launch something new. Maybe even to improvise a little craft. Tentatively, foolishly, yet with ardor, and an eye out for who or what, is seaworthy. In this place where I am. Nowhere else.

❦ SECOND ACTS ❦

2008

Some authors spend too much time on research. It's a stalling technique—a way to remain pleasantly immersed in a subject without actually writing about it. Months go by, deadlines pass, and still, these people shuffle around in obscure archives, following crumbs having fewer and fewer connections to the half-baked manuscripts languishing on their desks.

I am one of those shufflers, ever deluding myself that weak links to a subject will yield the real story, the whole song. Yet once in a while I hit on a lure that turns into an obsession that at least enlivens my spirit, if not the topic at hand. The most recent case of this started when I discovered the *Collected Works of Lafcadio Hearn* (Houghton Mifflin, 1922), all ten volumes, on a low, mite-infested shelf in the darkest room of a Texas library.

I'd been directed to Hearn (1850–1904) by a historian who knows I am working on a book about Louisiana's Atchafalaya River Basin, west of New Orleans. Hearn, my friend told me, lived in New Orleans from 1877 to 1888, writing for *Harper's Weekly, Scribner's Magazine* and two local newspapers: *the Daily Item* and the *Times-Democrat*. Some critics today, like Frederick Starr, editor of *Inventing New Orleans* (University Press of

Mississippi, 2001), a collection of Hearn's Louisiana pieces, suggest Hearn single-handedly created the Big Easy's exotic mystique by way of his colorfully observed descriptions of the people, culture, and landscape there. A few even trace Louisiana's modern tourist industry back to this odd little writer, himself of furiously exotic descent. But more of Patricio Lafcadio Tessima Carlos Hearn's origins later.

Since I'd come to Hearn by way of Louisiana, I was ignorant of his reputation as a writer on Japan, where he later lived. Just as he invented mysterious New Orleans, I learned, Hearn interpreted mysterious Japan for English-speaking readers. Intent on staying my original course, though, I set that fact aside and trolled Hearn's Louisiana work for Atchafalaya references, turning up little useful material. I should have quit him then, but as I've said, I am a staller.

Maybe it was because I was still in my American Buddhism phase (following my Walker Percy phase, my Jung phase, my Emerson phase and my D.H. Lawrence phase); anyway, I next alit on Kenneth Rexroth's *The Buddhist Writings of Lafcadio Hearn* (Ross-Erikson, 1977), a charming, insightful treasury of pieces about crickets and dew-drops, with as precise a description of the path to nirvana as I've read. In this collection, Hearn's voice differs markedly from that in his Louisiana writings, and I wondered if he had consciously undergone a transformation. The more I thought about it, the more I wanted to know why Hearn left New Orleans for Japan; I wanted to know what made this peripatetic writer tick.

So for more than a year, I trafficked in Hearn lit, haunting the life and work of a bookish fellow who was born in Greece of a Greek mother and Irish father, raised by an aunt in Ireland after his parents' divorce, and at nineteen, sent to

Cincinnati to seek his fortune. His was not an attractive visage; when Hearn was sixteen, an accident blinded and whitened his left eye, and his right eye bulged congenitally. He was slightly built as well, and altogether his appearance, mixed background, and intellectual disposition rendered him an outsider—the perfect stance for a journalist, which is what he turned himself into. In 1874 he was hired as a staff writer for the *Cincinnati Enquirer*, winning notoriety for lurid accounts of backstreet life. Three years later he was fired when his brief, troubled marriage to a half-black woman came to light. In 1877 he went to New Orleans on assignment for the *Cincinnati Commercial*, and stayed. Ten years after that, having sated himself in that city, he spent two years in the West Indies writing for *Harper's*. Once more, he grew restless and in 1890 moved with even less in hand to the other side of the world, where he eventually married into a traditional Japanese family, changed his name to Yakumo Koizumi, fathered four children, taught, lectured, and wrote prolifically. He died of heart failure in 1904 and was laid to rest in Japan.

Like his contemporaries Robert Louis Stevenson and Pierre Loti, both also born in 1850 and enamored of the tropics (as were artists such as Gauguin) Hearn traversed a wide swath of geography. Hearn was especially drawn to Loti's impressionistic, melancholy writings; he moved to Japan only three years after Loti's novel *Madame Chrysanthème*—a precursor to Puccini's opera *Madame Butterfly*—appeared. But unlike Stevenson and Loti, Hearn was not a grand Victorian traveler with ample means to globetrot. A freelance writer with no steady income, inheritance, or well-heeled wife, he lived from paycheck to paycheck. For him, moving to Japan was, practically speaking, like hurling himself off a cliff.

In his excellent book *Wandering Ghost: The Odyssey of Lafcadio Hearn* (Knopf, 1990), Jonathan Cott reveals Hearn to be a sensitive, complex soul, a passionate reader and autodidact interested in every little thing around him, like an eye to the hundredth power. *Wandering Ghosts's* form—a biography with substantial excerpts from Hearn's work—is apt, as Hearn was no mere reporter, but a stylist and story-teller. Through the excerpts I noticed how in Japan, Hearn gradually modulated his style from a blend of romanticism and impressionism to a less overwrought but no less passionate approach that heightens the individuality of whatever the eye falls upon. This fascinated me: the way moving from one land to another might affect the way one expresses oneself. The way one's voice might irrevocably change.

But did Hearn know what he was doing? Did he intentionally seek a make-over? Shuffling toward an answer, I staked out clear before-and-after comparisons. Here is an example of Hearn's pre-Japan prose from *The Garden of Paradise*, a piece in Starr's collection about the Bayou Teche country.

> It is the moss that forms the theme of the scenery—if a musical word may be used descriptively. It constitutes the character of the landscape. It is omnipresent and omnipotent in effect. It streams from the heads and limbs of the oaks; from the many-elbowed cypress skeletons it hangs like decaying rags of green. It creates suggestions of gibbets and of corpses, of rotten rigging, of the tattered sails of ships "drifting with the dead to shores where all is dumb." Under the sunlight it has also countless pleasant forms—the tresses of slumbering dryads, the draperies flung out upon some vast woodland-holiday by skill of

merry elves. Under the moon, losing its green, every form of goblinry, every fancy of ghastliness, every grimness of witchcraft, every horror of death, are mocked by it.

And then I found this excerpt from *In the Cave of the Children's Ghosts*, originally appearing in Hearn's *Glimpses of Unfamiliar Japan* (1894) and included in *Lafcadio Hearn's Japan*, a classic anthology edited by Donald Richie in 1997 and released again by Tuttle Publishing in 2007.

A tremendous line of dark iron-colored cliffs, towering sheer from the sea without a beach, and with never a speck of green below their summit; and here and there along this terrible front, monstrous beetlings, fissures, earthquake rendings, and topplings-down. Enormous fractures show lines of strata pitches up skyward, or plunging down into the ocean with the long fall of cubic miles of cliff. Before fantastic gaps, prodigious masses of rock, of all nightmarish shapes, rise from profundities unfathomed. And though the wind to-day seems trying to hold its breath, white breakers are reaching far up the cliffs, and dashing their foam into the faces of the splintered crags.

Gone in this excerpt is the reliance on personification, with the exception of the wind that "seems trying to hold its breath," and Hearn's obsession with the ghoulish, which marks so much of his work, is, but for "nightmarish shapes," suggested, not named. Yet the writing is no less dramatic. I wondered: was the change merely a response to a different physical environment? After all, Spanish moss drooping from

Southern oaks could invite the sort of hyperbolic expression Japanese cliffs might not.

Since the start of the millennium, Lafcadio Hearn's work has reappeared in several new collections and editions—evidence, perhaps, of a resurgent interest in Hearn's work, and the shadowy man behind it. Besides Starr's invaluable collection and the new edition of Richie's anthology, we have Delia LaBarre's *The New Orleans of Lafcadio Hearn: Illustrated Sketches from the Daily City Item* (Louisiana State University Press, 2007), a gathering of short takes on everyday life in New Orleans, with the cunning pen-and-ink scenes Hearn loved to dash off. One piece claims the mosquito "is a first class judge of dry goods, and distinguishes afar off the quality and thickness of socks and stocking. She poketh her little bill through the finest material that modern machinery can spin." Alongside is pictured an annoyed fellow in bed, a giant insect astride him.

And finally, apropos of my quest, there is *The Life and Letters of Lafcadio Hearn*, edited by Hearn's friend Elizabeth Bisland one hundred years ago, and reissued this spring by Wildside Press in three volumes. Browsing through them, I was attracted by the letters to New York Tribune music critic Henry E. Krehbiel showing Hearn's ambivalence about Louisiana, his discontent with American materialism, and the unmistakable *artistic* restlessness and ambition that ultimately drove him to Japan. Here are some key excerpts:

New Orleans, 1878

> One cannot write of these beautiful things while surrounded by them; and by an atmosphere, heavy and drowsy as that of a conservatory. It must be afterward,

in times to come, when I shall find myself in some cold, bleak land where I shall dream regretfully of the graceful palms; the swamp groves, weird in their ragged robes of moss . . .

New Orleans, 1883

. . . I think it more probable I shall see you here than that you shall see me there. New York has become something appalling to my imagination . . . When I think of it, I feel more content with my sunlit marshes,—and the frogs,—and the gnats,—and the invisible plagues lurking in visible vapours . . .

New Orleans, 1886

O that I were the directing spirit of some new periodical . . . devoted especially to the literary progression of the future . . . Then, wouldn't I have lots to say about The Musician,—*my* musician,—and the Song of Songs that is to be!

For my own purpose now lieth naked before me, without shame. I suppose we all have a purpose, an involuntary goal, to which the Supreme Ghost, unknowingly to us, directs our way . . . Well, you remember my ancient dream of a poetical prose,—compositions to satisfy an old Greek ear,—like chants wrought in a huge measure, wider than the widest line of Sanscrit composition, and just a little irregular, like Ocean-rhythm. I really think I will be able to realize it at last.

There was my treasure, my answer, my endpoint: proof of Lafcadio Hearn's intention to transform his voice—to give himself to his art. Four years later, he sailed off to Japan, not knowing how long he'd stay, and the rest, as they say, is history. Shuffling back to my desk, enriched by the side-trip and inspired by Hearn's courage, I set aside his books and began to write my own.

www.ingramcontent.com/pod-product-compliance
Lightning Source LLC
Chambersburg PA
CBHW021002090426
42738CB00007B/624